'This is a rare publication that brings together
authority of a writer who has been profession
educational enterprise. While this is not a "how
for new ways for schools to understand and pi
contribution is timely: he provides sensible, '
illustrations, as well as wise counsel from his yea
in the development of education when the pi
processes are keenly felt. Most significantly, he stresses throughout his book the vital
role of leaders in bringing about school development through research engagement.'

**Winthrop Professor Helen Wildy, Dean of the Faculty of
Education, The University of Western Australia**

'*Research Engagement* is a very valuable publication and I believe will prove to be a
significant contribution to the literature and thinking about practitioner research
and school research engagement. There is a continuing need to address the issues
related to the standing, status and credibility of practitioner research and research
engaged schools within the research community. This publication tackles this in-depth,
with a great degree of intellectual rigour and analysis. True to the very principles of
research it does this in a clear and balanced way and thereby makes the compelling
case for greater recognition of the research engaged school movement.'

**Graham Handscomb was Senior Manager, Stategic Development, Essex Local Authority,
UK and is now Managing Director of Graham Handscomb Management Services**

'*Research Engagement for School Development* offers a timely exploration of what it is for
schools to engage with research as consumers, facilitators, partners and producers. Raphael
Wilkins examines key issues for school leaders and potential change agents, including
the relative merits of centrally-directed and locally motivated enquiry; characteristics of
research that can usefully inform practice to make a difference in schools and classrooms;
the relationship between practitioner research and teaching as a professional form of
"clinical practice"; and leadership styles that facilitate research engagement within the
ethos of education as a human and humanising activity. A key strength of the book is
Wilkins's writing style, which combines serious scholarship with a high level of readability –
offering an account which manages to be both authoritative and thought-provoking, yet
an enjoyable read. The book draws upon the ideas of a range of commentators, whilst
offering a coherent analysis. Wilkins contributes to the literatures about teacher research
and school improvement in a way that teachers and school leaders will find informative
and empowering. Wilkins's final chapter sets out a plea for the importance of knowledge
about knowledge in informing thinking about research and schools. Wilkins has here hit
upon a key issue that deserves to be taken much more seriously. Engaging with research
without some level of epistemological understanding and analysis is akin to students who
study but fail to engage in meta-cognitive reflection upon their own learning. That is, such
naivety leaves educators inherently limited in their ability to critically engage with the
relevance and implications of research. This argument would by itself justify putting this
book on the reading list of anyone concerned with research in educational contexts.'

**Dr Keith S. Taber, University of Cambridge Faculty of Education and author of
*Classroom-based research and evidence-based practice: A guide for teachers***

'This book brings together recent theory, practice and policy on practitioner research. Raphael Wilkins is a rare example of someone with both academic scholarship and practical experience, bringing multiple perspectives to bear on the growing interest in reflective practice and research engagement. He explains the origins of research engagement in relation to research-utilisation and evidence-based policy-making, presenting detailed case studies of research by school leaders to illustrate the process, outcomes and constraints involved. The book poses some important questions about the ways in which research engagement can be more or less empowering, depending on whose agenda is served. This wide-ranging book should be of particular interest to those wishing to understand more about how teachers can get involved in research, to the benefit of their pupils, their schools and themselves.'

Caroline Sharp, Research Director,
National Foundation for Educational Research (NFER)

'This thorough, 360 degree exploration of the existing and potential contribution of research engagement to school development is both welcome and timely for those who work in this drastically changing landscape. One-hundred Teaching Schools in England have just been given explicit responsibility for engaging with and in research and encouraging this in those they support. They will also be involved in initial teacher education, continuing professional development, leadership development and school-to-school support. It may be that the growth of engagement with research as part of school development has reached a stage of maturity capable of taking advantage of the opportunities this clearing of the ground affords. It may also be that the private providers and third sector chains of schools newly emerging will also choose to explore these opportunities. But the terrain is as complex as the prize is great. Innovators hoping to take this work to scale will be need to have the confidence to work to longer timescales and more broad-ranging goals than have been the habit of the private sector or of groups of schools who are properly tackling very pressing challenges for particular students. What Dr Wilkins's book offers is a much needed, deeply considered exposition of some of the major issues that the new players on the scene will need to take into account, accompanied by a series of personal cases and examples to ground his analysis in practice and bring it to life.'

Philippa Cordingley, Chief Executive, Centre for the Use of
Research and Evidence in Education Ltd (CUREE)

Research Engagement for School Development

Research Engagement for School Development

Raphael Wilkins

Institute of Education, University of London
Issues in Practice

First published in 2011 by the Institute of Education,
University of London, 20 Bedford Way, London WC1H 0AL

www.ioe.ac.uk/publications

British Library Cataloguing in Publication Data:
A catalogue record for this publication is available from the
British Library

ISBN 978 0 85473 900 4

Typeset by Quadrant Infotech (India) Pvt Ltd
Printed by Elanders

Contents

Contents

List of figures

List of abbreviations

AERA	American Educational Research Association
BERA	British Educational Research Association
CANTARNET	Canterbury Action Research Network
CPD	continuing professional development
CUREE	Centre for the Use of Research and Evidence in Education
EPPI-Centre	The Evidence for Policy and Practice Information and Co-ordination Centre
FLARE	Forum for Learning and Research Enquiry
GTCE	General Teaching Council for England
HEI	higher education institution
ICT	information and communication technology
INSET	in-service education and training
LEA	local education authority
LGA	Local Government Association
LSIS	Learning and Skills Improvement Service
NCLSCS/NCSL	National College for the Leadership of Schools and Children's Services, previously the National College for School Leadership
NERF	National Educational Research Forum
NFER	National Foundation for Educational Research
NLC	Networked Learning Community
NQT	Newly Qualified Teacher
NTRP	National Teacher Research Panel
Ofsted	Office for Standards in Education
PISA	OECD Programme for International Student Assessment
PPD	postgraduate professional development
TDA	Training and Development Agency for Schools
TLA	Teacher Learning Academy

Acknowledgements

The author would like to thank all those whose experiences and perceptions have been drawn upon in this book, and those who have offered helpful suggestions during the writing, including in particular Judy Durrant, Graham Handscomb and David Frost.

The author and publisher are grateful for permission to use material previously published in the journals *Education Today* and *Professional Development Today*.

Preface

In keeping with the traditions of the practitioner research movement, I begin with a biographical summary of my own journey towards and through the territory of school research engagement, to explain how I have come to my current standpoint and particular range of interests.

My first batch of published articles appeared a dozen or so years into my career. I had been a teacher, and then an education officer, in three London boroughs, before spending a few years working with the House of Commons Select Committee for Education, Science and the Arts. There I saw at first hand, on a daily basis, one distinctive form of interface between expert knowledge and the policy process, and that experience made a lasting impression on my thinking. I went on to be the Education Officer of the Association of London Authorities, at the time when the Government was abolishing the Inner London Education Authority, and became active in parliamentary lobbying processes. The articles I wrote during that period included explorations of the relationship between research and policy (e.g. Wilkins, 1986a, 1988) and discussions on whether research findings derived in one setting could be applied to other settings (Wilkins, 1986b, 1987). I returned to local government, combining this with external interests: a visiting fellowship at the Institute of Education, University of London (IOE), a secondment to the then Department for Education and Employment, and continuing parliamentary lobbying work for the local authority associations. This was a period of change and financial retrenchment, and for a decade my professional and scholarly concerns shifted to focus on the field of strategic business management of education systems.

I was, in consequence, well into mid-career before discovering the practitioner research movement. I found myself in the role of Director of Education in Thurrock, a small, new unitary authority serving an area of chronic educational underachievement on the north bank of the Thames estuary. I had nine months to establish a team and to get ready for the smooth transfer of functions from the previous authority, whereupon I turned my attention to the conundrum of how to raise educational aspirations. This was in a context where many teachers and headteachers had very low expectations of their pupils, and equally low expectations of the new local authority, which was in large measure the previous district council. As one influential headteacher expressed it, 'The people who ran the dustcarts are now going to try to run schools'. It seemed to me that raising attainment would involve developing the professional culture, and one of the strategies I adopted for this was to set up a series of research projects to be undertaken by practitioners in schools and colleges, working in partnership with a local university. I felt a need to be effective in personally offering professional leadership and challenge, and to do that, following a long period in which I had been concentrating on management and policy, I returned in my reading to educational writings and found myself inspired and energised by them.

The Thurrock Local Education Authority (LEA) Research Project expanded to include academic support from two universities. Eight of the practitioner researchers involved presented their work at an international research conference, which was a significant achievement for them, as none of them had previously addressed an academic audience. I told the story of this project in Wilkins (2000a). There were some spin-offs: I gave the keynote address at the Canterbury Action Research Network (CANTARNET) conference (see Chapter 1) in 2000, and Thurrock was asked to pilot what was to become the Government's Teachers' International Professional Development scheme; I also represented the Local Government Association (LGA) as a Board Member of the National Foundation for Educational Research (NFER). Of the articles I wrote between 1999 and 2005, the majority concerned the relationship between practitioner research and school development, with an emphasis towards school leadership issues.

While that particular experience of leading a cross-phase practitioner research project is now in the past, I want to share some of the reflections I recorded at the time, because they shaped my understanding of issues that remain relevant.

At the start of this project, the intention of the team was that each practitioner researcher would negotiate their topic of enquiry to fulfil three criteria:

- It had to have direct relevance to that individual's priorities in their current work.
- It was desirable for the projects to share some points of connection, so that the sum would be greater than the parts.
- I wanted each project to relate to one of the local authority's functions. This latter was so that the research projects would be able to influence policy and to feed into evaluations of the authority's performance.

From the outset, being aware, from the Hillage Report (Hillage *et al.*, 1998) and my own earlier work (Wilkins, 1988), of longstanding debate about the gulfs between research, policy and practice, my intention was that the project could provide a demonstration of how those gulfs could be bridged at local level. The essence of the project was to use research both to improve practice and to influence policy. I thought that intention was clear to all parties and jointly owned, and in a general sense it was, but I did not devote sufficient attention to surfacing and exploring in-depth with the team how we should take account of it in the way we worked together. Some months into the project, at the point where research questions and foci of enquiry were being refined, I developed a perception that as a team we were living out in microcosm the same gulfs and tensions between research, policy and practice that are debated at national level. I represented policy, the practitioner researchers represented practice, and the university represented academic research. I felt that the team, as they refined their research questions through individual academic supervision, were not taking sufficient account of my needs as a policy-maker. At the same time, a number of the team, myself included, felt that this same process was not taking sufficient account of the team members' specific needs as practitioner researchers as distinct from conventional academic researchers. Working through these issues helped to clarify some aspects of the special nature of practitioner research.

Research engagement combines practitioner research with drawing upon and using published research findings. As well as leading the practitioner research project, I took a small and not at all premeditated step in the latter direction. As part of my own personal professional development, I attended the 1999 annual conference of the American Educational Research Association (AERA), which that year was held in Montreal. This was my first attendance at AERA or indeed at any conference devoted to research rather than to mixed or practitioner interests. Since then, I have attended and presented papers at numerous international conferences, but have never experienced again the sense of acquiring so much intensive learning, of growth, of new vistas opening, as I did on that first occasion. Fazed by a programme of telephone directory proportions, with over 3,000 individual presentations, I put off until I arrived the task of working out what I would actually do in Montreal. I did not go with any specific practical or policy problem in mind: that would have put my subsequent activity into a different model of research utilisation, i.e. the problem-solving model. Nor was I working on any sustained line of research of my own, that I planned to learn more about at the conference: that would have put me into the interactive model of research utilisation. With such an extensive menu of presentations to choose from, I decided I would learn more by concentrating on a particular topic, and into my entirely open mind formed the resolve to specialise in sessions on school, family and community partnerships. That decision put my subsequent activity into the research to practice model of research utilisation. There were about 50 presentations with a link to this theme, and I was able to listen to 30 of them. I found the format, commonly a batch of four or five papers on a similar theme, with a chair, a discussant and brief open forum, an effective means of gaining an overview of the issues and debates within the field. My review of these, and advocacy of one particular approach, the Epstein model of school, family and community partnerships, was published in 2000 (Wilkins, 2000b).

As a novice to the field, the Epstein model (Epstein et al., 1997) came to my attention in several ways. A number of the papers presented by other researchers made reference to Epstein's work, with some adopting this, with or without modification, as the conceptual framework for their own research. In two of the sessions presented by other researchers, Joyce Epstein herself spoke as discussant and as a contributor from the floor. One of the symposium sessions concentrated on reports by other researchers of activities specifically implementing the Epstein model of partnership. A team led by Joyce Epstein presented a paper (Epstein et al., 1999), providing an update of the pattern of involvement with her model at state and district levels (in the USA). The National Network of Partnership Schools at Johns Hopkins University had been set up in the 1996–97 school year to help schools, districts and state departments of education to develop research-based programmes of school, family and community partnerships, with states and districts in formal membership of the Network being expected to meet basic requirements for leadership, funding and support, and to use a common framework so that they could communicate with others about their work. The paper reported the activity of eight states and 53 school districts. Sanders and Simon (1999) presented a similar report of the activity of 375 elementary, middle and high schools in membership of the National Network of Partnership Schools. Brittingham (1999), a school district superintendent in Wisconsin, presented research he had conducted in six school districts in Wisconsin which had been identified as having made good progress in implementing the Epstein model of partnership.

By this time, my interest was seriously engaged, and I began to wonder whether this approach could usefully be applied within the UK context. The Epstein model recognises six distinct types of partnership: parenting, communicating, volunteering, learning at home, decision-making and community collaboration. It emphasises some key principles, which are supported by research evidence. Each type of partnership needs specific attention and a different approach. The respective roles of the partners differ between the different types of partnership. Schools, the local authority and other agencies can make a difference to the quality of each type of partnership, but this can only be sustained through a systematic programme of support and development. The Epstein model is presented in a handbook (Epstein et al., 1997) that also contains materials for supporting development projects.

At that time, the Epstein model was not unknown in the UK; it was cited by academics and known to some practitioners, but as with so much of the UK partnership scene there was an absence of the infrastructures necessary for the effective practical application of the model. The potential value I saw in the Epstein model was not any particularly distinctive theoretical merit over other work in the field, but rather that it was simple to understand and hence to apply in practice, and came with well-developed support arrangements for practical implementation, provided through the National Network of Partnership Schools at Johns Hopkins University. The model thus provided a suitable basis for an overarching framework for development projects, and appeared user-friendly for policy-makers and administrators.

Following my return from the AERA conference (at the end of April 1999), I organised an internal conference for senior staff of the Education Department, to report on the visit and to raise discussion of how the information and ideas I had gathered might be applied to the schools in our local authority. The conference took place in July 1999; it was for half a day and 32 senior staff took part. My role was to make the main input in the form of an oral presentation, and to organise group discussions. Colleagues compiled a set of detailed notes and planned actions, which at that early stage included mapping existing provision, auditing practice against the Epstein model, and staff development.

Having discussed the issues at officer level, I arranged an informal seminar for elected members of the Learning Services Committee to share my ideas and to establish whether or not there would be political support for policy-making. This seminar took place in July 1999. Meanwhile I was in e-mail correspondence with Joyce Epstein about the options and possibilities for becoming the first school district outside the USA to make a formal commitment to this partnership model (which did happen), and whether it would be practicable to formalise a relationship with the National Network of Partnership Schools (which in the end I decided not to pursue).

Towards the end of July 1999, I reported formally to the Learning Services Committee on the potential benefits of the Epstein model. I requested (and obtained) permission for the local authority to:

- adopt the overarching framework (of the Epstein model)
- commend the framework to schools, agencies and partners
- promote the sharing of good practice in each of the six types of partnership
- produce a newsletter to raise awareness of school, family and community partnership issues
- produce good practice guidelines for how each type of partnership could be applied to the corporate parenting of children looked after by the local authority

- identify in consultation with schools priorities for professional development to support aspects of partnership work
- establish a local authority forum for discussing school, family and community partnership issues
- explore and establish appropriate external alliances to support the work. The latter was to empower me to continue discussion with Johns Hopkins University and with potential UK university partners.

In September 1999, I started disseminating some explanatory materials about the Epstein model to schools, as part of the preparation for a focus on this theme at a headteachers' conference in February 2000. A concurrent development was the launch of a school-based MA programme of supported practitioner action research, and I designated partnership with parents as a focus which would receive particular encouragement and support. Several teachers in middle leadership positions took up that option. At the February conference I gave keynote and workshop inputs on the subject, and asked schools to volunteer to join a pilot project to implement the Epstein model.

In March 2000, I reported again to the Learning Services Committee, requesting and receiving permission to support a series of school-based pilot projects to implement aspects of the Epstein model. Ten primary schools and five secondary schools took up this opportunity. A project support team of six relevant postholders was designated to provide advice, materials, in-school and local authority meetings, training and co-ordination. Leaflets were produced and meetings took place, including well-attended sessions to share and support the development of practice which took place in October and November 2000. I left the service of the local authority at Christmas 2000, and at that point, despite the departure also of certain other champions of this policy, the momentum appeared to have become established. Over a period of 18 months, enough had taken place to embed the initiative.

From January 2001, I began a freelance period which I used to pursue wider educational interests and to complete my doctoral research. For that I studied a group of school leaders, drawn from across England, who had personally engaged significantly in practitioner research. The aim of my research was to explore their perceptions of how their practitioner research activity had affected their approach to their leadership role. While undertaking this research, I was working with the (then) Canterbury Christ Church University College as one of the tutors of an accredited school-based practitioner enquiry programme (MA in School Development) led by Judy Durrant, which had previously been established by David Frost who moved from Canterbury to Cambridge University. I was also working part-time as Education Policy Adviser at the Local Government Association. In the latter capacity I had the opportunity to contribute advice that formed part of the process of commissioning the NFER to undertake two major research projects in this field. The first was a study of the role of local authorities in using research for school improvement (Wilson *et al.*, 2003).

The second research project commissioned in this way was the National Research Engaged Schools Project, led jointly by NFER, LGA, the General Teaching Council for England (GTCE), the then National College for School Leadership (NCSL) and five individual local authorities, which began in 2003. This project grew out of the work of Handscomb and MacBeath (2003), who initiated the term 'research-engaged school', and specifically from discussions between Graham Handscomb, who at the time was at Essex County Council, and Caroline Sharp of NFER. I was a member of the Steering Group for this project (representing the LGA) and had the pleasure of working with the key figures in the field, including Handscomb, Sharp and Lesley Saunders. Looking around the table at the first meeting, I thought it would have made a good case study of the role of policy entrepreneurs: a distinct impression that most of those present would have been there regardless of the organisation to which they were currently affiliated.

This is the point at which it is appropriate to make a transition from a personal narrative to more scholarly discourse on the development of the research-engaged schools movement, which I have continued to study and support since joining the IOE in 2006.

Like Mockler (2007), I am conscious of the shortcomings of which I could be accused in writing some of the thoughts and memories that I share in this book. For authenticity, I present not only knowledge drawn from scholarship and research, but also some of my 'knowledge' of my own thoughts and perceptions. Running alongside the academic presentation of lines of argument, readers will catch frequent glimpses of the continuation of the personal subjective story begun in this preface.

Raphael Wilkins
May 2011

About the author

Dr Raphael Wilkins is Assistant Director (International Consultancy) and Director of International Affairs in the London Centre for Leadership in Learning, Institute of Education, University of London (IOE), and is also President of the College of Teachers. Before joining the IOE in 2006, his career included teaching; education officer roles in four local authorities including over 12 years in Chief Officer level posts; national roles with Parliament and the local authority associations; six years of senior level consultancy, research and writing; and attachments to a number of universities. At the IOE, Raphael has managed a wide range of leadership development projects and programmes in the UK and internationally, and he has undertaken consultancies in India, Singapore, China, Yemen, Saudi Arabia, Southern Sudan, Pakistan and Mexico. Raphael has published over 50 articles and research reports, has led many workshops on leadership issues, and has presented papers or keynotes at education conferences in Britain, Denmark, The Netherlands, Cyprus, Canada, USA and China.

Chapter 1

Research-engaged schools

Introduction

'Knowledge is power'. This book explores that traditional maxim in relation to how people who work in, and with, schools use knowledge to 'power' the process of improving the quality of education. It is concerned with two sources of knowledge in particular: knowledge created by undertaking school-based practitioner research; and knowledge accessed by school personnel from published research findings. In both cases, these forms of knowledge are supplements to, not replacements for, the professional judgement which should always form the bedrock of teachers' work.

The profession of education has been going on for a long time, and is centrally concerned with the aim of obtaining and using knowledge. It might be assumed that these relationships between knowledge and practice would already be so clear as to require no further comment. It might be assumed that the fields of school-based practitioner research, and engagement with published research findings at school level, would be characterised by broad agreement about the nature of the activity, the purposes to which it should be directed, and to what extent and by whom it should be 'policed'. In fact, these are contested territories, in which there are different standpoints, reflecting significantly different underlying viewpoints about the nature of teaching as a profession, and the role of schooling within society. There are different views about what counts as 'high-quality education'; about the processes which lead to school improvement; and about the nature and status of the 'knowledge' that teachers can generate through practitioner research.

This book aims to draw attention to and explore these different standpoints, so as to provide a map on which readers can locate their own preferred positions, and can also identify the positions of key individuals with whom these matters are debated or who seek to support schools in particular ways. Everyone has a position (which may of course develop over time), and there can be no such thing as 'neutrality' in relation to some of these issues, so the positions adopted in this book are made explicit at relevant points.

There is another reason for beginning with the maxim 'knowledge is power'. Practitioner research, one of the two main arms of school research engagement, is an act of intervention, intended to lead to changes in practice as well as to changes in the perceptions and self-confidence of those who undertake it. Rarely can it be value-free; rarely, at least at the micro-level, can it be apolitical. Individual teachers or school leaders conducting their own practitioner research will often be conscious that, whatever other motivations and intended outcomes may be driving the activity, their engagement in it affects their standing in their organisation in one way or another, often through increased influence or specific career development, or possibly even by presenting a challenge to elements of the organisation's leadership. Practitioner research that is officially supported, for example by school leaders or by agencies within the local school system, is a distinctly political activity, which often is fully intended to have an impact on power relations. It enables individuals to take control of the issues in their own situations and to address them. It promotes a view of teaching and school leadership as research-based professions in which the influence of research is partly bottom-up rather than almost wholly top-down. It offers the prospect of empowered and evidence-based local school system leadership. It will be argued later in this book that the practitioner research movement could develop the scale and impact of its operations to the point of having greater influence on policy debates at national level.

This book adds to the literature on research-engaged schools, by seeking to fill a gap at the meeting point between five different 'literatures': bodies of writing that, while related and overlapping, tend to have their distinctive central concerns, fields of scholarship and bases of evidence. These are:

- methods books on 'how to do your practitioner research project'
- books that promote teacher-led school development and present and celebrate its products
- the currently growing new field of writing on the specific notion of 'research engagement' by schools
- books on the ways in which research influences policy and practice
- books on school improvement and school leadership (really several different fields but for simplicity here treated as one).

To appreciate the deeper issues of school research engagement, it is necessary to make the connections with all of these surrounding literatures and, hopefully, to achieve an overall coherence. One of the success criteria for that might be to achieve clarity not just on the 'what?' and 'how?' of school research engagement, but also on the 'why?' and 'to what ends?'; perhaps even 'to whose ends?'.

So this is not a methods book ('how to do your practitioner research project'). Instead it sets out an argument for looking in new ways at research engagement by schools as a dimension of school development. It is intended to be of interest to those many within schools and universities who affiliate themselves with the 'practitioner research movement'.

It is intended also to be of interest to reflective school leaders, and those who work supportively with schools in advisory roles, who are not personally research-engaged but who believe in its benefits. To these groups, the book may help to clarify the 'point' of research engagement and the manner of its linkage to school development, and perhaps generate new ideas about how to support the growth of effective practice in this field.

This book is also intended to be informative for school staff taking higher degrees in education, especially the many Master's programmes which include a significant school-based research component, for university staff teaching or supervising practitioner research elements of higher degree programmes, and for senior school staff preparing for headship, in addition to a general readership among those concerned with education policy and leadership.

The book draws on the author's experience of supporting school-based practitioner research and research engagement over a 12-year period, both as a senior system leader and policy adviser, and in university roles. Over that period (1998–2010) there have been some significant changes to the practice of school-based research:

- First, the incidence of teachers undertaking practitioner research and reflective action planning of the kind championed by David Frost (see, for example, Frost *et al.*, 2000) has increased considerably, and has become more diversified in style and approach (and hence, to some extent, in depth). Groups of teachers working in this way have become established sub-sets of the professional culture of some schools.
- Second, and partly as a natural consequence of the first development, there is now in schools a cadre of researcher-leaders: headteachers with substantial personal experience of undertaking practitioner research who promote and support it as part of their leadership function (see, for example, Wilkins, 2002).
- Third, the research-engaged schools movement, championed especially by Handscomb, has strengthened the connections between small-scale practitioner research projects, and the more general body of education research activity (Handscomb and MacBeath, 2003).
- Fourth, debate about the impact of research has continued (see, for example, Saunders, 2007), and since the election of the Labour Government in the UK in 1997 there has been a greater incidence of governmental claims that policies are 'evidence-based'.

The activities encompassed within school research engagement represent a significant investment of resources: by schools (and by individuals working within them); by universities and local authorities; by the General Teaching Council for England (GTCE) (specifically in relation to its Teacher Learning Academy); by the Training and Development Agency for Schools (TDA) and the National College for the Leadership of Schools and Children's Services (NCLSCS).

Then apart from investment in research engagement, there is the much greater investment in education research itself. Most forecasters of public spending are predicting the onset of an extended period of financial constraint, in which climate many schools and other budget-holding organisations will, regrettably but perhaps understandably, see investment in research engagement and in related staff professional development as having a lower priority than core functions. Even people very much in favour of school research engagement would acknowledge that this is a good time to be subjecting the activity to critical appraisal.

What is a research-engaged school?

In the sense in which the term is used in this book, a research-engaged school has the following three characteristics:

- It undertakes its own research through a significant incidence of good quality internal practitioner research.
- It accesses research findings from external sources and takes these into account in its work.
- It is willing to be the subject of research undertaken by others.

In addition to these three characteristics, three further attributes should be added: first, that these characteristics are sustained through the impetus of the school itself, rather than because the school is being 'done to' by external agencies; second, that these characteristics have significant bearing on the professional culture of the school; and third, that the school has an outward-looking professional orientation.

In their pioneering work, Handscomb and MacBeath (2003) defined research-engaged schools as those that have a research-rich pedagogy and a research orientation, promote research communities and place research at the heart of their outlook, systems and activity, so that:

- significant decisions are informed by research, by this being built into organisational systems
- people have access to tools that challenge their practice, by the development of research skills being built into the school's professional development
- others have access to sufficient detail about how research was conducted in order to make their own judgements about it

- the outcomes of research are effectively communicated within and beyond the school (Handscomb and MacBeath, 2003).

Sharp *et al.* (2006a) defined a research-engaged school as one that:

- investigates key issues in teaching and learning
- uses enquiry for staff development
- turns data and experience into knowledge
- uses evidence for decision-making
- promotes learning communities.

To appreciate fully the meanings conveyed in these definitions, it is necessary to look at accounts of what schools have done, such as those in *Postcards from Research-Engaged Schools* (Sharp *et al.*, 2005), or the well-established and ever-evolving work led by Graham Handscomb through FLARE, the Forum for Learning and Research Enquiry, which has, for example, produced a resource pack for helping children to develop their research skills (Essex County Council, 2009). In reality, within the fledgling, dynamic field of school research engagement, there are not yet any discernible schisms of belief about the nature and purpose of the activity. However, it is necessary to go a little further than these definitions in clarifying the concept and in recognising issues, such as the long-running debates within the practitioner research movement more generally.

Headteachers might wonder about the thresholds that apply to these criteria, and about the extent to which the claim 'we are a research-engaged school' is one of those self-designations that say as much about the interests and mindset of the school leadership team as about the facts of actual practice. If a school is a 'good' school, addressing its issues in a thoroughly professional manner, with plenty of staff development, with the staff keeping up with professional reading, going to conferences and engaging in dialogue such as through 'learning communities', does its progression to being able to call itself a 'research-engaged school' involve some marginal enhancements of practice or something more fundamental? Or if a school is heavily committed to internal practitioner research and is happy to share its outputs, is that a sufficient condition for saying that it is a research-engaged school? Laudable though that practice might be, something more than undertaking practitioner research is implicit in the notion of the 'research-engaged school' that is currently emerging. That is why the start of this chapter put forward the view that research engagement also implies actively utilising published research findings.

There were times during the growth of the school practitioner research movement when some of its proponents took a stance that presented teachers' action research as independent from, not needing, and alternative to, research undertaken using other methodologies. Jean McNiff's *Action Research:*

Principles and practice (McNiff, 1988) is one example, although McNiff's later writing moved away from that position. It was possible for a school to be heavily involved in teachers' action research in a way that not only was disconnected from the wider world of education research, but also in other respects had an inward-looking focus. This is still possible. So it is preferable for definitions of research-engaged schools to be clear that undertaking internal practitioner research is a necessary but not sufficient condition.

'Turning data and experience into knowledge' is one of the criteria in the definition offered by Sharp *et al.* (2006a). Anyone new to the field will naturally want to know how to do that. The answer is found partly in published examples of research engagement, but it also depends partly on the dynamic relationship between these three concepts of data, experience and knowledge, which, according to how 'knowledge' is defined, might be understood as overlapping concepts. This raises the central issue, which has been the subject of long-running debate, of the nature and status of the 'knowledge' produced through practitioner research engagement, and, specifically, whether and in what circumstances it achieves the status of 'research findings' as understood by the academic community. It will be argued in Chapter 5 that school-based personnel can go about their research engagement in ways that will maximise the 'knowledge status' of their outputs.

'Investigates key issues of teaching and learning', also a criterion in Sharp's definition, may appear to be such a reasonable assertion that many readers may be surprised by the following argument that this statement illustrates one of the 'issues' in school-based practitioner research. It was noted earlier that there are different viewpoints about the nature and extent of practitioner research that should be 'allowed' to take place. The easiest way to illustrate this is to draw caricatures of 'managerial' and 'professional' stances towards teaching:

- Those adopting the 'managerial' perspective tolerate practitioner research, provided that it is subject to top-down control, and focuses on improving certain narrowly defined performance indicators in ways which help 'management' to achieve its objectives. In this perspective, 'key issues of teaching and learning' can be code for 'quick fixes to measured attainment to improve league table position'.
- Those adopting the 'professional' stance will see practitioner research as an integral aspect of being a teacher; as an activity that is largely self-directed, broad in scope, and that over time might take the school's thinking forward on questions such as what is a 'good education' and in what new ways aspects of that might be assessed.

These are just caricatures, of course, and not for a moment implying that Sharp and her team subscribe to a managerialist standpoint, which they do not; only that their form of words could be interpreted as endorsing such a view. This book is positioned firmly towards the 'professional' end of the continuum. In a research-engaged school, and bearing in mind also that nearly half of all the people who work in schools are not teachers, there is no reason why the areas of school life improved through practitioner research could not range across the whole operation, for example including the pastoral care and well-being of children, home–school relations, extra-curricular learning, the development and management of the school site, resource deployment, liaison with other agencies, the introduction of a coaching culture, the professional development of staff, and, of course, the 'key issues of teaching and learning'. As part of that mix, it is also only natural that from time to time, staff may want to do something primarily to help themselves get on in their career.

Using published research findings

The second strand of school research engagement is the use by schools of published research findings. The key factors in determining the value of this activity are how, to what extent, and to what ends published research findings are deployed. School staff need to be as discriminating in their application of these external resources as they would of any other. As with zealous converts to a belief, those new to school research engagement need to guard against assumptions that all research is good and useful, and that research provides answers to a wider range of school development issues than is in fact the case.

There are four main reasons why research-engaged schools will find it helpful to access published research findings:

- This provides essential contextualisation for the school's internal practitioner research, which needs to be approached with prior knowledge of the relevant field.
- As a form of general professional development, research reports form part of professional reading, and can stimulate fresh thinking about practice. In some subject areas on some occasions, research findings can help to inform the approaches that are taken to specific school development issues.
- Familiarity with, and confidence in using and critiquing, published research findings will help the school to appraise claims by external change agents that their initiatives are 'based on research'.
- Some schools see an additional benefit of taking an interest in research findings, as being the opportunity to model the behaviours they advocate to students. If school staff are spending much of their lives persuading young people that it is good to use sources of information to address the issues in their lives, and supporting them

in developing the skills to do so, then it is logical that they will wish to be good role models, demonstrably enjoying and benefiting from their own learning.

Not many schools have the capacity to sustain effective engagement with published research findings on their own. In reality, members of staff who are studying for higher degrees form the main group of school-based personnel reading research reports in any kind of regular and systematic way. Where schools, as part of their professional development policy, are supporting batches of staff in undertaking advanced study on an ongoing, rolling basis, this can provide a spine around which a critical mass of research engagement activity by staff more generally can be sustained. Most schools wanting to engage purposefully with published educational research findings will benefit from external support from any combination of networks with other schools, support from the local authority, and support from one or more higher education institutions. In Chapter 7 a case is made for the importance of ensuring that the dynamics of those relationships are conducive to building the capacity of the school.

White (2007) comments on how the National Teacher Research Panel (NTRP), established by the UK Government in collaboration with the General Teaching Council and the (then) NCSL, undertakes a number of activities which support the different strands of research engagement by schools, and, in doing so, helps to strengthen the concept of the research-engaged school as presented in this book. The NTRP has held a biennial conference on best practice in practitioner enquiry for around 500 teachers and headteachers, which aimed not only to enable participants to learn from each other how to undertake robust action research, but also to learn how to access and use published research findings. (At the time of writing, the future of NTRP and its conference are uncertain.)

Integrating research and experience

At an individual level, learning is bound up with experience. The process of making sense of the world includes stages that are essentially individual and personal. Practitioners in education have their unique combination of experience, perceptions, prior learning, beliefs, and what they have retained from professional and academic reading. Through acts of intellectual creativity, they form their own patterns from these disparate items of knowledge: patterns that will work uniquely for them. While other people's conceptualisations, even those of distinguished authors, can provide important starting points in stimulating understanding, they are not completely transmittable from one mind to another without a process of taking ownership, which involves reinterpretation, and the imposition of new nuances of meaning, which derive from the recipient's own thoughts and experience.

Research engagement involves practitioners' thinking being influenced by academic research. If that influence is to be supported, the processes whereby practitioners identify the connections between what they experience and what they read become matters of interest in their own right. In order for those processes to be understood, it is important that practitioners are given every encouragement to articulate their intellectual journeys as honestly as possible. It is easy and tempting to allow the benefit of hindsight to endow intellectual journeys, retrospectively, with standards of orderliness, logical sequencing and purposefulness that go well beyond the reality.

In real life, some actions are taken, or positions adopted, instinctively, which later are found to be consistent with rational argument – a process that begins with unconscious association, a sense that certain approaches or ideas 'go with' certain others. Individuals exemplify the characteristics of Ranson's learning society (Ranson, 1994) as they progress from unconscious to conscious learning, as they discern coherent patterns connecting knowledge from different sources, and as they relate the learning they undertake to their capacity to address the issues in their lives.

This progress is not necessarily smooth. Professional interaction, networking and conference attendance produce chance encounters and fragments of information and ideas. Reading may commence at the margins of a field and only later discover seminal works. Small incidents may engender significant new insights. Immediate priorities affect decisions about which sources of information will receive attention. If productive dialogues are to be developed among those involved at the meeting points of research, policy and practice, then the disjointed nature of individuals' intellectual journeys should be shared and understood, rather than regarded as shortcomings to be disguised.

What is practitioner research?

Cochran-Smith and Lytle (2007) identified a range of activities falling within the broad definition of what they termed 'practitioner enquiry'. These include:

- action research
- the use of teaching as a context for research
- the scholarship of teaching and learning (i.e. using reading as a research method to make one's practice more research-informed)
- a group of activities that in the UK would usually be described as 'reflective practice'. These activities include: 'teacher research', in which teachers use enquiry communities to examine their own assumptions and to develop local knowledge; 'self-study' –

continuously interrogating one's own practice and its assumptions; and 'narrative enquiry', which is (autobiographical) writing produced through systematic reflective practice, that contains 'knowledge', and that is 'a way to uncover and represent teachers' personal practical knowledge' (Cochran-Smith and Lytle, 2007: 26).

To count as 'enquiry', all of these activities need to be both intentional and systematic. It is a feature of practitioner enquiry that the 'research' element cannot be separated out from the practice, posing some problems in the application of the normal rules of research ethics, which are addressed in Chapter 5.

The components of Stenhouse's (1983) definition of research as 'systematic and sustained enquiry made public' might be opened up as follows.

Systematic and sustained

- The process of enquiry is conscious.
- The enquiry addresses clear questions.
- It has a sense of purpose and timescale.
- Documentary records are maintained.
- The enquiry is linked to relevant research literature.
- Attention is given to authenticity and trustworthiness.

Made public

- The enquiry is discussed with colleagues.
- It is the subject of contributions to conferences and networks.
- Documentary records are accessible.
- Reports are made available.

The central element of Stenhouse's definition, 'enquiry', is examined in Chapter 5.

The research-engaged schools movement

The research-engaged schools movement arose out of the practitioner research movement, which in schools in the UK traces if not its origins, at least a significant early boost to the work of Lawrence Stenhouse cited above (Stenhouse, 1983). Stenhouse promoted action research by teachers, and provided the definition of research as 'systematic and sustained enquiry made public', which is loved by practitioner researchers because it affirms that their enquiry activity 'counts' as research. Promoting a definition that something is the case did not, of course, in itself end the debate surrounding that issue. This early development of school-based action research and its association with the curriculum development of the period is recorded by Burton and Hartlett (2005).

Action research became one accepted means of undertaking the dissertation element of taught higher degree programmes. Interest grew in the more extensive accreditation of practitioner research by teachers. As part of that development, David Frost introduced the MA programme at Canterbury Christ Church University that incorporated his approach of 'reflective action planning'. The course was entirely school-based, with the support of an external academic tutor, but required a viable peer group led by an in-school co-ordinator, generating a critical mass of teachers working in the same way and acting as a mutually supportive learning community (Frost *et al.*, 2000). This format of Master's programme delivery, requiring collective engagement at school level, was an important step from research-engaged individuals towards the notion of a research-engaged school. Frost also established the Canterbury Action Research Network (CANTARNET) as a wider learning community and support group for this approach to school development. These developments at Canterbury continued under the leadership of Judy Durrant, with an emphasis on teachers' leadership of change (Durrant and Holden, 2006).

After Frost moved to Cambridge, one of his projects was the Hertfordshire Learning Partnership with a group of schools in Hertfordshire, which is described by McLaughlin *et al.* (2006). This combined school-based enquiry and learning communities with specific strategies to support schools in applying relevant research findings in areas such as assessment for learning (Black and Wiliam, 1998). This combination of action research with the use of published research was a clear early example of school research engagement. In 2002, the original project grew into the larger Herts-Cam Network, which is still flourishing.

Meanwhile, in Essex County Council, Graham Handscomb had established the Essex County Council Forum for Learning and Research Enquiry (FLARE), which developed a strong local authority supported infrastructure to schools around the issues of enquiry, networking and research engagement, including thematic attention to topical issues. With John MacBeath of Cambridge University, Handscomb pioneered the current concept of the 'research-engaged school' (Handscomb and MacBeath, 2003).

Lesley Saunders, Policy Adviser for Research at the GTCE from its creation until 2009, ensured that from the outset the GTCE sought to be an evidence-informed organisation, and promoted research engagement by teachers. She ensured a strong contribution from GTCE to the National Research Engaged Schools Project. That project generated most of the recent spate of writing on research-engaged schools, including the project report itself (Sharp *et al.*, 2005).

Does research make a difference?

Chapter 2 explores whether, and in what ways, research makes a difference to education policy and practice. The purpose of this is to set the subsequent treatment of research engagement by schools within the context of the broader relationships between research, policy and practice, and within the context of debate about the purpose and usefulness of educational research.

The models of research utilisation derived from utilisation studies including the work of Weiss (1986) provide conceptual frames of reference for clarifying a number of aspects of research engagement. In covering this ground, an overview is provided of the debate about the influence and usefulness of education research, and how the education research community, and government, have responded to criticisms of educational research in the Tooley and Hillage Reports (Tooley and Darby, 1998; Hillage *et al.*, 1998), and in David Hargreaves's lecture to the Teacher Training Agency (Hargreaves, 1996). The question is raised of how the growth of the practitioner research movement, and research-engaged schools, may be affecting the dynamic of the interfaces between research, policy and practice, perhaps calling for a reappraisal of some well-worn assumptions.

Linked to that debate is the extent to which it makes sense to talk about 'transferable good practice' in teaching. It will be argued that this notion has limited application, and should not be used as a yardstick against which to judge the appropriateness or quality of practitioner research. Finally, a start is made in Chapter 2 on the issue of the contribution of practitioner research to the growth of knowledge.

Evidence-based reform

Chapter 3 explores further the notion of 'evidence-based reform' – a form of research utilisation which, while capable of carrying a range of interpretations and applications, is mainly associated with a desire to promote the top-down imposition of the results of certain forms of educational research, especially those bearing the characteristics of large-scale 'scientific' experiments. This chapter identifies the theoretical and practical problems presented by that approach, and the issue of managing the interface between 'top-down' and 'bottom-up' approaches to research utilisation by schools.

Why do school leaders become research-engaged?

Much of this book is concerned with rational and normative arguments in favour of research engagement by schools. These are, however, tempered by empirical considerations, by looking at the viewpoints of research-engaged individuals. Chapter 4 uses case study examples of the 'authentic voice' of research-engaged school leaders to illustrate a range of different reasons and motivations for school leaders becoming research-engaged. These personal accounts highlight the linkages between research engagement and broader educational beliefs and values, and in particular, the ways in which school leaders' values and beliefs affect school culture. They also illustrate the multiplicity of benefits sought and realised by these champions of research engagement: research is not just to solve problems, but it can be a way to model beliefs and values, to lead and develop staff, and to promote teacher-led reform.

How worthwhile is practitioner research?

While there are good reasons to advocate school-based practitioner research, it would be unwise to make any generalisations about its quality or worth. So much depends on what is done and how it is done; why and to what effect. Supporters of this activity need to recognise and respond to some genuine problems about the status of the 'knowledge' produced through practitioner research. This applies especially to accounts that are essentially reflections on practice.

One can read reports in which a teacher describes a development or process of change, dressed up with the language of 'investigation' and seasoned with academic references, but leaving doubt about whether the teacher's actions or understandings were in any way altered by their purporting to be 'doing research'. If research, following Stenhouse, is 'systematic and sustained enquiry made public', then it has a genuinely fuzzy boundary: at what point does reflective recording of normal professional practice demonstrate sufficient qualities of 'systematic enquiry' to qualify as 'research'? Just as there is a point at which travel writing may upgrade into anthropology or geography, so there will be a point at which accounts of reflective educational practice may acquire the status of educational research. The account itself should contain sufficient information to enable the reader to judge whether that transition has occurred, and in the Stenhouse model, the account ('making public') is ongoing rather than only through summative reporting.

For example, a member of staff of a local authority education department submitted an analytical account of a change in which she had been involved, as part of a higher degree programme. The work received a high grade from the university. It was an impressive piece of academic writing. The only problem from the point of view of other people working in her organisation, was that it bore little relation to reality. Anyone actually involved in the change would suspect that the individual writing the report had delusions of grandeur about both the significance of the change, and their own reportedly leading and pivotal role in bringing it about. Yet that report might be accessed by a future researcher and taken at face value as evidence of 'practitioner-led reform'.

A valid question in relation to some outputs of practitioner research in education is the extent to which it is reporting real things, as distinct from reporting the perceptions and state of mind of the individual by whom it was undertaken. 'Why should anyone believe you?' is a legitimate challenge. In good practitioner research, which deserves to be taken seriously, the answers to that question will be evident from the report, especially in relation to the range of viewpoints accessed and the extent to which the researcher's interpretation of their findings has been validated.

Chapter 5 makes some suggestions for the successful practice and management of school-based practitioner research, including ways to increase the credibility and usefulness of its outputs, and to manage the ethical issues that it can raise.

Does it all depend on the attitude of the headteacher?

One of the recurrent themes in supporting and writing about school-based research is the extent of variation between schools as suitable environments for adopting the research-engaged approach. The organisational cultures of some schools are supportive to this, while others are hostile. Given the high level of school autonomy and emphasis on school leadership which characterise the English system, it is inescapable that the attitudes of the headteacher and other members of the senior leadership team are among the main factors which cause this variation.

Chapter 6 offers a series of pointers, derived from scholarship and practice, towards effective and sustainable support by school leaders for research engagement in schools. This exploration covers support by leaders for research engagement for its own intrinsic merits and as a process for managing school development. It also shares some examples of how research engagement can be used by school leaders to achieve a number of beneficial human resource management outcomes, such as the motivation, retention and development of staff. The approach to this discussion covers the relationship of research engagement to education leadership literature, and the relationship between research engagement and school development. It then looks more specifically at how headteachers support research engagement, stages in the development of 'researcher-leaders', and aspects of leadership that school staff cite as being conducive to research engagement.

External support for research engagement

It is not easy for a school to be self-sufficient in its research engagement activity. That is why an outward-looking orientation needs to be one of the attributes defining the research-engaged school. Schools need those wider connections to provide intellectual stimulation and challenge, to facilitate access to information and research findings more efficiently, and to access specialised support, including academic advice and accreditation. The dissemination of the school's practitioner research also requires a network.

Chapter 7 emphasises the outward-facing orientation of research-engaged schools. It provides an overview of some recent developments and initiatives, to illustrate how the dynamic of these relationships is changing, and could change more. In the early days of school-based practitioner research supported by universities, the role of the school was either purely permissive, enabling individual members of staff to undertake higher degree programmes that incorporated a research component, or, where a more specific role was involved, the school was very much the junior partner in the arrangements. Much good may come from that, and in many situations that will be the only practicable option. But the designation 'research-engaged school' should be reserved for schools which have progressed from a passive, 'done to' or junior partner role to a proactive partnership of equals. Chapter 7 envisages the school as being in the driving seat, setting its own agenda, rather than responding to the agenda of the partner organisation. Such a school will understand what forms of external support are available, and which will best match its needs. It will have the confidence to manage the process of procurement or collaboration.

Research engagement: Whose agenda?

Chapter 8 returns to the theme of the range of positions, stances and agendas being pursued at every level and in every corner of the field of school research engagement. This argument is illustrated by examples of educational beliefs and values, by the school improvement agenda, by the agendas of activist research, and by the contexts of globalisation and innovation. Chapter 8 argues in favour of the leaders of research-engaged schools developing heightened awareness of all of the various 'agendas' being pursued within the field, so that they may more consciously and confidently select and advance their own standpoints.

Approach taken in this book

This book presents several distinctive lines of discussion.

Its focus on research engagement as a concept adds to a fledgling field, and helps to establish the connections between the related literatures of practitioner research, school development and research utilisation.

Incidentally, there is a reason for choosing the words 'school development' in the title of this book. Writing which emphasises the search for proven replicable practices, often with a focus on detailed practice inside classrooms which implements externally derived solutions, has often been associated with the label 'school effectiveness'. Writing which emphasises broader processes of beneficial change, which may be externally supported but which are institutionally led, with teachers and school leaders playing a significant part in devising their own solutions, has often been associated with the label 'school improvement'. The term 'school development' is intended to embrace both of those traditions. For an overview of the interrelationships between these fields, see White and Barber (1997). The link to models of research utilisation is that school effectiveness will tend to prefer the research to practice model, while school improvement will tend to prefer the problem-solving and interactive models of research utilisation.

From the standpoint of research engagement, the book revisits in a supportive but critical way some of the longstanding issues regarding school-based practitioner research, including its quality, usefulness, knowledge status and impact. It makes a case for taking the development of practitioner research from a predominantly small-scale, individual activity to additionally embracing larger-scale projects using a wide range of research methods.

This book gives attention to the relationships between research engagement, school leadership and organisational culture. It explores the wider meanings of research engagement, including its alignment with certain beliefs about the nature of teaching and the purposes of education.

Chapter 2

Relationships between research, policy and practice

School leadership teams choosing to use research engagement as a means to support school development may want to have a considered view of the role of research, not least so as to be able to articulate this when the topic arises in discussions with staff. This view might cover issues such as the kind of contribution that research can bring to decision-making; whether research findings have greater practical utility in relation to some aspects of school life than to others; and the proper balance to be struck in decision-making between what research appears to be saying, and the exercise of normal professional judgement. To support such position-taking, this chapter provides an overview of, and a commentary on, the main lines of debate within the education research community about the relationships between research, policy and practice.

This chapter also sets the treatment of research engagement by schools in subsequent chapters within the context of the broader relationships between research, policy and practice, and the context of debate about the purpose and usefulness of educational research. It presents models of research utilisation in order to provide conceptual frames of reference for exploring a number of aspects of research engagement.

The majority of writings in this field fall into one or more of three foci of interest:

- Over a period continuing to the present time, but most intensively during the 1980s, studies have been conducted of the extent to which research (usually large-scale projects) has influenced policy-making by governments, and the factors that have helped and hindered that relationship.
- A second strand, running from the late 1990s to the present, takes the form of responses from the education research community to criticisms by government and its agencies, and prominent individuals (notably David Hargreaves), that the research it produces is less useful than it ought to be.

- A third focus of writing concerns the beneficial relationship between practitioner research and educational practice.

This debate has been ongoing since the 1980s, and the thoughts that follow select those aspects of it that are of most relevance to people working in research-engaged schools today. Where the focus of writing is on the impact of research, this has often tended to bracket together impact on policy and practice. There is a pattern in more recent writing to treat as separate subjects, raising separate theoretical concerns, the impacts of research on policy and on practice. For those who have spent much of their careers working on the interface between policy and practice, and wanting naturally to keep both equally connected to the issue of research impact, it is natural to react instinctively against this. Yet there is an obvious practical utility to this separation.

From the viewpoint of a research-engaged school, the impact of research on policy (or more specifically, the kinds of policy-making dealt with in these writings) is mainly just a matter of wider contextual interest and background information, whereas the impact of research on practice is something that schools can actually change through their own actions. There is a significant distinction between engaging with one field through professional reading, and another field as an actor helping to shape what that field is discovering. There is, however, a factor that complicates that distinction somewhat. David Hargreaves pointed out that the decision of David Blunkett, as Secretary of State, to make professional practice the direct target of policy-making ended the convention by which politicians remain distant from classroom practice, and in these specific fields, evidence-informed policy and evidence-informed practice became conjoined (Hargreaves, 2001: 204–5).

National debate about educational research

A surprisingly large amount has been written on the subject of the debate about educational research which took place in the few years following 1996. In 1996, David Hargreaves gave a lecture at the (then) Teacher Training Agency on *Teaching as a Research-Based Profession* (Hargreaves, 1996), which proved controversial among the education research community. Readers coming new to this field may be impatient with a debate which took place over a decade ago, but the substance of the debate represented a battle between different lines of reasoning. To some small degree it is reminiscent of the Reformation, in which understandings of beliefs were unpicked and challenged in ways which meant they could never be quite the same again, but ever after defined in relation to coordinates of schism.

An engaging treatment of the debate is that of Martyn Hammersley (2002). Hammersley's own research background was in ethnography, which, with its concern to understand the meanings that different people ascribe to the phenomena they experience, is pretty much at the opposite end of the spectrum from the mechanistic 'what works, one right way' school of educational research. Hammersley did, nevertheless, adopt judiciously balanced stances in his commentary, and offered an enjoyable thoroughness of scholarship with which he set the debate within its historical context.

Hammersley (2002) traced the sequence of events following Hargreaves's 1996 lecture, which criticised university-based educational research, and advocated more research of the kind that would enable teachers to adopt something similar to the evidence-based practice typical of medicine. The following year (1997), a new Labour Government came to power, which through a range of behaviours indicated more interest than its predecessor in evidence-informed policy and practice. In 1998, the Government's Department for Education and Employment (DfEE) published the Hillage Report *Excellence in Research on Schools* (Hillage *et al.*, 1998), and the Office for Standards in Education (Ofsted, the Government's inspection service) published the Tooley Report *Educational Research: A critique* (Tooley and Darby, 1998). Hammersley related how Charles Clarke, then Parliamentary Under-Secretary at the DfEE, led a series of initiatives in 1998 to respond to the issues raised by these reports, including the creation of the National Educational Research Forum; the establishment of the EPPI-Centre at the IOE ('EPPI' is short for 'Evidence for Policy and Practice Information and Co-ordination'); and encouragement for the development of centres of excellence. The presentation of these policy developments made clear the emphasis that the Government wished to place on the practical usefulness of research (Hammersley, 2002).

The debate about educational research sparked off by Hargreaves and the Tooley and Hillage Reports involved position-taking on who has the right to define what educational research should be, and the criteria by which its usefulness should be judged. The Hillage Report was based on four strands of evidence-gathering, which included interviews with 40 key stakeholders. Others took part in discussion groups or submitted written papers. Looking afresh today at the list of contributors, it is striking how balanced it was, including many champions of practitioner research. The report itself, commenting on perceptions among practitioners of a general lack of impact of research on policy and practice, stated that practitioner action research was the exception, and several positive examples were cited. The report's treatment of the barriers affecting research utilisation is fair and moderate and, in large measure, still remains applicable. Its conclusion rests on a judgement, which could never be derived entirely from empirical analysis, that the impact of research 'ought' to be greater than it was. Few people would disagree, but the question which is central to this debate is: what level of impact is it reasonable and realistic to expect to be able to achieve?

The Tooley Report began life with the disadvantages (from the point of view of how it was received by the education research community) that it was commissioned by Ofsted, and that its foreword by the then HM Chief Inspector of Schools, Chris Woodhead, was characteristically provocative and opinionated. The report itself, for the most part, still makes an interesting read regarding the approach taken to critiquing educational research as a field. Less palatably, it critiqued to the point of ridicule, as from some standpoints it is easy to do, certain examples of writing within positioned genres, rather in the way that some gallery visitors like to laugh coarsely at Picasso's paintings. As part of the method of conducting the review, a checklist of 30 questions was developed, and then applied to articles in four selected journals. With one proviso, the core 13 of these questions continue to be useful for any practitioner researcher, or reviewer of a published research report, to keep in mind, and they are reproduced in the box below.

Box 2.1 Research review checklist based on the Tooley Report (Tooley and Darby, 1998)

- Does the research involve triangulation in order to establish its trustworthiness?
- Does the research avoid sampling bias?
- Does the research use primary sources in the literature review?
- Is the relevant literature adequately surveyed?
- Does the research avoid partisanship in the way it is carried out and in the interpretation of data?
- Is the research conducted by practitioners, or informed by their agendas, and/or presented in such a way as to be accessible to them?
- Is the argument coherent and lucidly expressed?
- Do the conclusions flow from the premises and argument?
- Are unfamiliar terms adequately defined and assumptions clearly set out?
- Are concepts used consistently?
- If controversial empirical and non-empirical propositions are introduced, is their controversy acknowledged, and arguments given, or referred to, to justify supporting the proposition?
- Is the presentation of the research such as to enable questions about the conduct of the research to be adequately explored?
- Does the presentation of the research avoid partisanship?

This selection from the full list of questions (some of which concerned factual information about the particular piece of research) includes the avoidance of partisanship, which seemed particularly important to Tooley's thinking. The proviso referred to earlier is that partisanship cannot be completely avoided in any research in a field like education (for example, it may have influenced the choice of topic to examine), even if care is taken not to reveal it. So it may be preferable to ask whether and how partisanship has been acknowledged and dealt with.

The Tooley Report's conclusions presented a mixed picture, which included criticisms of the quality and usefulness of the examples of research analysed. It is, however, important to emphasise that the review did not set out to answer, and from its research design could not have answered, a number of key questions. Yet the report allowed itself to imply a position in relation to these questions, and in that respect perhaps it came near to breaking its own strictures about partisanship. Specifically, the Tooley Report did not:

- attempt to investigate the actual level of impact of any of the examples of research critiqued
- establish that there is any general correlation between the quality of research (as defined) and its level of impact
- establish that the shortcomings in quality (as defined) of the examples of research critiqued acted as barriers to their impact
- establish that, had the quality (as defined) of these specific examples of research been higher, their impact would have been greater.

These key questions not having been addressed left the Tooley Report's findings firmly in the domain of opinions and wishes. Its key conclusion seems to have been that educational research *ought* to be of higher quality (as defined), and that research of higher quality *ought* to have more impact. Given the wide range of factors that act as barriers to research impact, and given that practitioners and policy-makers as the users of research are likely to be less forensically discerning about its quality than the research community, that conclusion did not take understanding of research impact very much further forward.

Models of research utilisation

A route into the matter of research utilisation (and hence to position-taking on how and in what ways research can be 'useful') is the seminal work of Carol Weiss (1986), which offered seven models of research utilisation. Set out below is a conceptual framework built on a simplified version of Weiss's models. Weiss's seven models were as follows:

1. linear, or pure to applied
2. problem-solving
3. interactive
4. political (i.e. selective use of research to support views held normatively)
5. tactical (e.g. to delay a decision)
6. enlightenment
7. research as a reflection of society's interests.

In the context of research about education (Weiss's analysis was based on a wider field) and the specific interests of research-engaged school leaders, the number of distinct models can be reduced. The seventh, in contrast to the first six, treats research as a dependent variable, which while raising interesting issues (what topics do research-engaged schools study and why) is a side issue. 'Enlightenment' is perhaps better understood as concerning the nature of research impact (in contrast to 'engineering' – see below), rather than as a model of research utilisation. For simplicity, 'tactical' can cover a range of circumstances including what Weiss described as 'political'.

In the comments which follow, 'ideas/knowledge/research findings' are grouped together to suggest that for the research-engaged school, 'research utilisation' is more accurately understood in practice as embracing wider notions of knowledge transfer than might be implied by a strict interpretation of the words 'research findings'. Also, in this analysis 'research' includes practitioner research, and this approach puts on one side for the moment the issue of whether all of the beneficial products of practitioner research claim the status of research findings. It is possible to recognise four kinds of 'directly interested parties' which may be involved in the transfer of knowledge. There are, of course, other indirectly interested parties, such as agencies concerned with quality assurance and governance. Some of these, in certain situations, might be the 'agency' referred to in the framework below, or one of the 'other sources'. So the framework proposed recognises four main interested parties:

- practitioner sources of ideas/knowledge/research findings
- other sources, including academic
- users of the ideas/knowledge/research findings (who may be practitioners or policy-makers)
- agents involved in the process of transfer.

The framework also recognises four models of research utilisation adapted from Weiss (1986):

- research to practice, in which the driving initiative comes from 'producers' of knowledge, who wish to see it disseminated and applied
- problem-solving, in which the driving initiative comes from potential users who are actively seeking out 'solutions' to a problem they have identified
- interactive, in which 'problems' and 'solutions' are identified concurrently in a context of collaborative professional working
- tactical, in which the driving initiative comes neither from producer nor user, but instead from an agent for whom the utilisation of the research supports a wider strategy.

Figure 2.1 illustrates these relationships in simplified form. Arrows indicate the direction of the driving initiative.

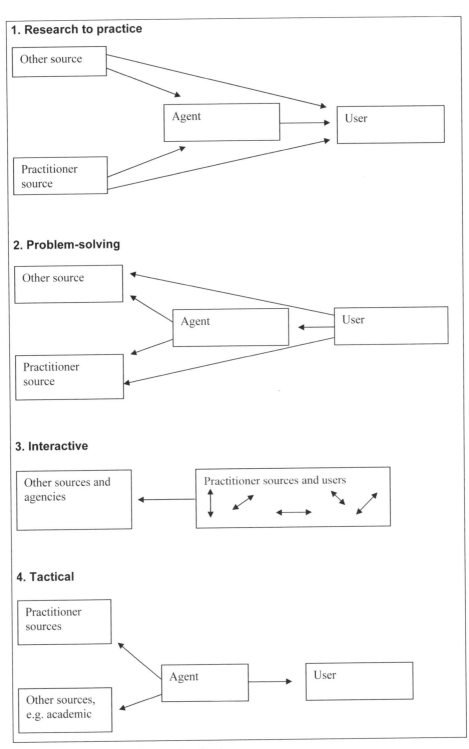

Figure 2.1 Four models of research utilisation

Research to practice

Figure 2.1 illustrates the different dynamics of the relationships represented by the different 'flows' within each of the models of research utilisation. The research to practice model occurs at multiple levels in the stream of research utilisation that starts with pure theoretical research and ends with ultimate practical application. Weiss's name for this model, 'pure to applied', emphasised the upper reaches of that journey, where pure, theoretical research receives its first processing into applied research. In the field of educational research, apart from some specialised topics, the length of that stream is not quite as extended as it might be – for example, between 'big physics' and the technician in the laboratory. This is because so much of the academic research on education collects its data from places and people involved in the practice of education, rather than in a laboratory. Even where its primary purpose is to build theory, it will often be talking about things that practitioners can understand and relate to.

The essential feature of the research to practice model of research utilisation is that the onus is on the producer of the research to get it disseminated and to see that it has some impact. This applies whether the research in question concerns the theoretical interests and pursuits of academics, or whether it is a substantial project commissioned by government to add knowledge in a general way to a topical area of concern (or a concern that was topical at the time the research was first commissioned!). The question for the researcher and their sponsor is what to do with research findings which emerge as outputs of knowledge-generating activity pursued either for its own sake (as in the case of academic research to advance theory), or for reasons other than the very directly expressed interests and needs of most of those who are now being pressed to read it. From the viewpoint of those at the receiving end of this model, the research simply appears as the result of publication and dissemination.

Increasing attention is being given to dissemination. It is now normal for funders of research to expect the work commissioned to include dissemination activity, and also for representatives of potential users to have been consulted during the research design process. Researchers are increasingly expected to be able to demonstrate the impact of their research: this is one of the measures in the new Research Excellence Framework, a mechanism for analysing the comparative standing of universities' research, which will affect how much funding universities in the UK receive.

When research-engaged schools find themselves on the receiving end of research to practice dissemination activity, they will obviously want to approach that with an open mind and a desire to learn, but at the same time, they need to be aware that the fundamental motivation for the activity is the researcher's need to secure some demonstrable impact for their particular research. In the research to practice model as conceptualised, the research is not purporting to be matched to the potential user's specific needs and circumstances, so the onus is very much with the potential user to judge its relevance and helpfulness.

Problem-solving

In the problem-solving model of research utilisation, the flows of initiative are in the opposite direction. The distinctive feature of this form of research utilisation is that the potential user of research has a problem (a policy problem or a practical problem) which triggers them to initiate a search for research findings that will help to solve the problem.

The problem-solving model can include newly commissioned research, for example where a government agency has a very tight and specific question to which it wants answers and commissions research intended to fill that gap in knowledge. An aspirational vision for the future of research-engaged schools could certainly include on the menu of possibilities the commissioning of problem-solving research by a school or group of schools, perhaps from a partner university.

Normally, however, the problem-solving model of research utilisation is concerned with finding 'answers' from the body of research that already exists, rather than with commissioning new, original research. The way in which this is done will vary according to the size of the organisation and the significance of the problem. At the micro-level, it might involve an individual in spending some time on the internet or in a university library. A good guide to this process is provided by Keeble and Kirk (2007), who suggest how to map the concepts, and offer practical advice on how to conduct searches and how to evaluate the material produced. Another helpful exposition is the chapter on 'Finding supportive literature' in Bauer and Brazer (2012).

Such searches may take the solution-seeker to summaries of research on the particular topic, such as those published by the EPPI-Centre at the IOE. Research summaries, overviews, digests and reviews of reviews are part of the contemporary infrastructure of research dissemination. The issues they raise are explored further in Chapter 3. The problem-solving model of research utilisation will often involve the 'solution-seeker' in a mixture of tactics, including their own professional reading, and identifying and seeking the guidance of expert individuals or of organisations specialising in particular issues.

Interactive utilisation

This type of research utilisation is exemplified by school-based action research and other forms of practitioner research and supported reflective practice, in which an evidence base is generated by learning communities of practitioners in the course of their work. At this micro-level, 'solutions' and 'problems' develop hand in hand, with the constant reframing of the 'problem' through the action research cycle.

This model differs from the other models of research utilisation in two important respects:

- In the other models, there is almost always a temporal separation, in which 'research' has to precede 'utilisation', whereas in the interactive model, these two activities proceed more or less hand in hand.
- In the other models, there is an assumption that the 'producers' and 'users' of the research are separate communities, whereas in the interactive model, both activities are undertaken within the practitioner community.

Frost has argued against the mindset in which practitioner research might drift towards other research traditions in ways which would lessen both of these distinct characteristics (Frost, 2007). Two particularly well-developed exemplifications of the interactive model of research utilisation are Frost's own work in teacher-led change (for example, Frost et al., 2000), and Handscomb's work through FLARE (for example, Handscomb and Smith, 2006). Both of these are discussed more fully in Chapter 7.

Tactical utilisation

The tactical use of research can be a controversial topic, and can raise questions about whether it is an entirely ethical activity. Tactical utilisation of research might, for example, take the form of gathering evidence to support a policy position that has already been adopted on normative grounds. That may sound like a clear misuse of research. On the other hand, everyone, even quantitative researchers, have stances on issues, and researchers tend to undertake research from their particular standpoint and focus of interest. Sometimes policy-makers want to know whether what they want to do has the backing of at least one group within a contested field, i.e. is consistent with one such standpoint. That does not in itself seem reprehensible: it might become so, if they then give the impression that the policy is 'research led' rather than 'consistent with one body of research opinion'.

Other examples of the tactical use of research are where it is deployed partly for an ulterior purpose, such as to engage participants in developmental activity, or to raise the profile of an issue. Here, the research is undertaken or accessed partly to achieve outcomes beyond the findings of the research itself. For example, where headteachers encourage and support school-based practitioner research projects, that may be not only because the outcomes are expected to be useful, but also to encourage the development of the professional culture of the school, to motivate staff to undertake professional development more generally, and to set good role models for students. It may also form part of strategies for recruitment, retention and succession planning. Research findings may also be highlighted tactically with a conscious intention to challenge complacent attitudes and to spark debate. Thus in some tactical uses of research, the ends are honourable and no-one is being deceived.

Research utilisation and the rise of practitioner research

The models of research utilisation derived from the work of Weiss (1986) and other writers of the period (e.g. Thomas, 1985; Finch, 1986) were based on analyses of large-scale conventional research projects across the social science field. At that period, and in the scope of such studies, practitioner research was not a relevant consideration.

The educational world of the current time presents a different landscape. First, the sheer volume of practitioner research activity has grown and continues to grow. A significant proportion of school leaders will have personally engaged in projects that they themselves classify as practitioner research, even though that may embrace a broad continuum of rigour, depth and value. Second, because most serious reading of research findings by school-based personnel is undertaken by people studying for higher degrees, many of which include a practitioner research component, there is an overlap between the groups 'potential users of published research findings' and 'practitioner researchers'.

Conventional thinking about the interfaces between research, policy and practice is also upset by a third factor, which is the growth of school autonomy. Despite what may have felt like a long period of central government prescription of how schools in England are to conduct themselves, it remains the case that the school is the place where many decisions about practice are made. According to the view that is taken of 'policy', it is also the case that, nested of course within national policy-making, schools have scope (and indeed a duty) to make policies in relation to areas of their responsibilities. Conventional depictions of the interfaces between research, policy and practice take it as given that the researchers, policy-makers and practitioners are three different sets of people who communicate poorly with each other, pursue different agendas and operate to different timescales (see, for example, Caplan *et al.*, 1975). While those issues continue to play out at the national level, at the local level school leaders in research-engaged schools combine in their own person the three identities of researcher, policy-maker and practitioner. Through their learning communities and networks, they form with like-minded colleagues a critical mass of individuals, each of whom combines those three perspectives. Projecting this development into the future, it is difficult to see how it cannot have a beneficial impact on the larger-scale dynamics of research utilisation.

At present, the interactive model is the model of research utilisation most closely associated with the practitioner research movement. Where a school has formalised its commitment to practitioner research, the problem-solving model also applies, in a form in which the 'sources' may include or even emphasise practitioner research sources. Examples of the tactical model include the encouragement of practitioner research by a school's leadership team as a means of developing the professional culture of the school; and local authority support for 'research engagement' as a vehicle for school improvement. Currently, practitioner researchers only feature significantly in the research to practice model as 'users' rather than 'sources' of research findings. Increasing the impact of practitioner research will involve upgrading its contribution as a 'source' in the research to practice and problem-solving models of research utilisation.

Chapter 5 will argue that this is likely to require a diversification of the forms of research design used by practitioner researchers, to include larger-scale projects using a wider range of research methods.

The nature of research impact: Engineering or enlightenment?

The sections above have looked at the forms or patterns of relationship between research and policy and practice. It is also necessary to consider the actual nature of the research impact arising from those interactions.

Patricia Thomas described the 'limestone' model of research impact, comparable to the way in which rain falls on and permeates limestone, emerging eventually as a stream after an untraceable journey. This she contrasted with researchers, independent of government, with the stature and inclination to act as 'gadflies', and with those researchers who use their connections as 'insiders' (Thomas, 1985).

A common distinction is between 'engineering' and 'enlightenment' models of research impact. Hammersley (2002) described the former thus:

> The 'engineering model' of the relationship between research and practice portrays research as directed towards finding or evaluating solutions to technical problems.
>
> (Hammersley, 2002: 22)

Hammersley separated 'enlightenment' into strong and moderate models:

- Strong enlightenment saw rationalisation as a process of historical development, and science as a worldview that can govern practice.

In this respect it is similar to the engineering model: both downplay the role of accumulated practical wisdom and assume science has a high level of validity.

- Moderate enlightenment by contrast gives research a more limited role in relation to practice, and its use depends upon practical judgements.

Hammersley also identified a 'cognitive resources model', which assumes a much weaker and less determinant relationship between the products of research and policy-making or practice. This sees the researcher as a contributor to bodies of knowledge which may be used as a resource by practitioners, but only as and when the practitioners judge appropriate, and with consequences that are far from completely predictable (Hammersley, 2002: 96). He pointed out that research impact is not always positive:

> Research-based knowledge is a resource which can be used to improve people's lives, but it can also be used to serve sectional interests, and purposes that most of us would judge to be evil. So there is often room for reasonable disagreement about what is desirable.
> (Hammersley, 2002: 46)

These models of research impact cast the researcher in different roles. In the engineering model, the researcher works as an aide, setting out to produce specific information that meets the requirements of policy-makers and practitioners. The researcher has the role of moderniser, supplying a 'scientific' way of thinking to replace the folk or craft methods that have previously been employed. In the enlightenment model, the researcher has the role of 'specific intellectual', supplying facts and/or arguments that can be used to challenge the status quo. The researcher as a 'public intellectual' provides a perspective that offers a new theoretical understanding of society, to replace the ideological view built into what currently passes for common sense (Hammersley, 2002: 93).

David Hargreaves (2001), in a thorough historical overview of these issues, referred to Robert Lynd's (1939) distinction 'between the *scholar*, who is at risk of becoming remote from life, and the *technician*, who is in danger of accepting policy makers' definitions of social problems and their short term solutions' (Hargreaves, 2001: 198). He also cited Gouldner's (1965) distinction between the engineer and the clinician as models for applied social science, noting that generally the engineer can take their client's definition of their problem at face value, whereas the clinician needs to make their own independent diagnosis of their client's problem. Hargreaves recognised that some conventional expectations about the impact of research on policy were simplistic, not taking account of the complexities of the relationship between policy-making and research. Those expectations were also founded on a 'naive positivism' regarding the extent to which social scientific theory could be generalised:

> Today the crude linear and positivistic model once assumed by many applied social scientists is patently naive...The motives of policy makers have many sources and their decision making is based on a wider range of influences and interests than just relevant research.
> (Hargreaves, 2001: 198–200)

Research impact on practice

The comments above about the nature of research impact provide a good basis from which to address the question: to what extent is it reasonable to assume that educational research should have direct and tangible impacts on practice?

In his commentary on David Hargreaves's criticisms of educational research, Hammersley (2002) drew attention to a number of fundamental difficulties regarding the extent to which educational research can provide trustworthy answers to practitioners' problems. The nature of the education process does not lend itself to 'positivist' research, partly because of the difficulty of establishing causal patterns in social phenomena. Hammersley highlighted the difficulty of identifying 'distinct and standardised treatments in education', and, at the receiving end, the difficulty of researching the processes of learning: 'the most important kinds of learning – relating to high-level, transferable cognitive skills or to personal understanding – are extraordinarily difficult to measure with any degree of validity and reliability' (Hammersley, 2002: 20). Even if these aspects of learning could be measured, the process of teaching and learning involves so many complex interactions and contextual variables that it would be extremely difficult to 'prove' causal relationships in a way that is comparable with the natural sciences.

John Elliott, one of the great champions of action research in education, critiqued (with Paul Doherty) some of Hargreaves's assumptions about the precise nature of the impact of research on educational practice (Elliott and Doherty, 2001). They saw in Hargreaves's writings a desire for educational research to generate 'decisive and conclusive evidence', yielding 'actionable knowledge of what works, couched in terms of statistical probability', like clinical trials in medicine. They also saw, paradoxically, Hargreaves maintaining that research evidence informs rather than displaces professional judgement:

> There appear to be two trajectories of meaning in Hargreaves' writings. On the one hand, 'actionable knowledge' provides 'conclusive and decisive evidence of what works'. On the other hand it is knowledge that informs the teacher's judgement of what works. Here it is the

teacher who decides whether the evidence 'constitutes actionable knowledge'.

(Elliott and Doherty, 2001: 216)

Elliott and Doherty considered that Hargreaves's methodological standpoint, while preferring quantitative research, accepted as useful the practice of educational action research by teachers of the kind advocated by Stenhouse (1983), but that Hargreaves regarded this as producing knowledge that is only private and personal, not knowledge that is 'actionable' generally, because it is neither generalisable nor cumulative. Yet:

Teachers have used case studies to inform their own judgements and decisions – a process known as 'naturalistic generalisation'... Teachers have also examined their practices in the light of formal generalisations about the condition of teaching and learning across a range and variety of contexts. Generalisations of this kind are developed by the application of methods of comparative analysis to case study evidence. Such methods are quite different from those of statistical aggregation. They attend to relationships between factors evidenced within a range of contexts, as opposed to establishing a general relationship by isolating factors from their context. Teachers' action research studies have been used as a basis for generalisation in both of the above senses, and have demonstrated that they can support the development of a professional, as opposed to a personal and private, knowledge base.

(Elliott and Doherty, 2001: 217–18)

Practitioner research as professional development

The professional development benefits of engaging in practitioner research are significant, and cannot be left out of any consideration of the impact of practitioner research on educational practice. This may be explained, in part, by reference to Popper's 'three worlds' (Popper, 1999). Popper termed the natural physical world as 'World 1', and the world inside the human mind as 'World 2'. He used the term 'World 3' to describe the products of the human mind, including physical artefacts and products such as institutions, and also intellectual artefacts such as theories and ideas.

This way of thinking might be illustrated by the way in which creative artists develop a relationship with their own creations. A mental image, in World 2, will become something new and different when set down on paper as a World 3 artefact. That artefact will engender a mix of reactions, including pleasure, disappointment, surprise, ideas for further work, and a desire to move forward and create more artefacts. It is natural to suppose that people who only ever create pictures in their minds are unlikely to develop artistically as much as those who create them in reality. It is not just an issue of the technical proficiency which can only grow with practice, but more importantly the growth of ideas and insights. One of the important differences between Worlds 2 and 3 is that the contents of World 3 are public and shared. They are of a form to which their creator and third parties can react; part of the creative stimulus which people derive from placing things in World 3 comes from being able to share them with others.

In schools, World 3 is much in evidence, for example in the curriculum and in educational resources. Teachers add to World 3 all the time in the course of their work. What distinguishes practitioner researchers is that their contribution to World 3 includes more material at their own intellectual level, and at the boundary of their own knowledge and understanding, than is yet the norm within the ordinary professional practice of teaching. There is no reason to suppose that the thinking of practitioner researchers is in any way superior to that of their colleagues. The difference is the extent to which private thinking (World 2) is carried through into a World 3 contribution. There are other kinds of World 3 contribution that teachers can make, which would have similar developmental value, such as writing books or presenting advanced professional development programmes.

When teachers talk about their practitioner research, it is often apparent that their practitioner research was, among other things, a form of expressive creativity. This does not in any way lessen its professional and theoretical significance. The point is that through their research, as with the expressive arts, teachers find a range of benefits: deeper personal identity, greater sense of agency, and the joy of making sense of the world and sharing their interpretation of it with others. These psychological factors have an impact on the overall performance of people in their professional role, which has to be recognised in any judgements made about the overall value of practitioner research. This also has a bearing on the mechanisms through which practitioner research affects practice.

How practitioner research affects practice

Middlewood *et al.* (1999) wrote about the benefits of practitioner research, that is to say, its efficacy in bringing about school or college improvement. They did not dwell noticeably on the problem of disaggregating the impact of the research itself from the impact of the researcher. Their accounts concentrated on the good developments which flowed from the examples of practitioner research presented. The same stance was taken by Halsall (1998) in his treatment of similar material, which emphasised the relevance of teacher-led development to school improvement.

Yet the effects of a particular piece of practitioner research on the context in which it was undertaken, if that is the researcher's normal working context, are almost always difficult to distinguish as a separate and independent factor from the effect of the practitioner researcher through their practice and as a person. This applies especially where the practitioner emphasises enquiry as a feature of their practice, and the research is integrated into their normal way of working. For that reason, it may be helpful to reconceptualise 'the impact of practitioner research' as 'the impact of practitioner researchers'. This acknowledges that in most practitioner research situations in schools, the 'research' cannot be dissociated from the 'researcher'. The personal involvement of the researcher is one of the distinguishing features of practitioner research, but the influence of the researcher, as distinct from the research, is also an issue in other research traditions. In a study of how research influences policy, Mitchell (1985) concluded that personalised knowledge had an important role. It was researchers rather than research, scientists rather than science, who had the greatest influence on policy-makers. Hargreaves's (2003) propositions tend, in contrast, to assume that 'research' can be treated as a commodity disembodied from the researcher, and that 'innovation' can be traded separately from its innovator. In relation to practitioner research, both assumptions are open to question.

Limitations to the lateral spread of 'good practice'

In *Education Epidemic*, Hargreaves (2003) argued for a new approach to education reform, in which the emphasis should shift from top-down direction by the UK national government, to the lateral sharing of information about good practice:

> We must all acknowledge the limits of central interventions and capitalise rather on the power and commitment of the professionals and others with local knowledge to work the magic that makes a sustained and disciplined transformation.
>
> (Hargreaves, 2003: 19)

There is much in *Education Epidemic* that can be read as supportive of teacher-led reform, and against top-down direction. Throughout, Hargreaves argued for less central direction, and in the latter parts of Chapter 7 described engagingly 'the babbling bazaar', free interchange of ideas, and sentiments opposed to mechanistic views of education. Yet much of his argument in earlier chapters seemed to assume a highly mechanistic understanding of 'innovation', and a highly directed system for deciding which innovations would be the most worthwhile. It is difficult to see how Hargreaves's version of the vision for teacher-led reform could be operationalised without considerable top-down management.

If one of the purposes of research is to provide solutions to problems, it is necessary to explore where the 'problems' come from for which 'solutions' need to be found. In the absence of such exploration, there is the possibility that the combination of small-scale practitioner research projects, school networks, and the lateral spread of innovation, might be focusing on the symptoms rather than the underlying causes of educational problems.

Many problems for education policy and practice are generated by asynchronous changes among linked factors. In an open society (Popper, 1966; Wilkins, 2010) there may be rapid changes in the expectations, aspirations, attitudes and values which make up society's normative context. The rapid pace of change within the normative context means that within the space of a decade, thinking which was regarded as at the fringe can become mainstream. The institutional pattern of formalised structures, laws, regulations, financial and decision-making arrangements changes more slowly, and at any particular time is likely to reflect the values and aspirations prevalent some years previously. There will be tensions between the institutional pattern and the current expectations of government and society. The extent of those tensions will depend in part on how far the political pronouncements of government run ahead of its ability or inclination to implement genuine systemic changes.

Too much reliance on practitioner networks and the lateral spread of 'good practice' could divert attention from the need to reform the institutional pattern itself. This emphasis could gradually slide into the message 'Look at how some teachers are managing to cope with these problems: if you network with them, then so can you', rather than recognising that some of these 'problems' are system-generated, and that classroom teachers should not have to cope with them to the extent that they do.

Part of this book's argument is that there are rational connections between seeing value in practitioner research, and holding certain views about how schools and school leaders should operate. This rational coherence embraces matters of epistemology, educational philosophy and politics. The constructionist epistemology with which practitioner research is associated sits naturally with a strong sense of human agency. If people have a part to play in the construction of meanings, based upon culturally transmitted concepts, but mediated through personal experience, observation and reflection, then it follows that people have a part to play in other things also, including taking control of the issues in their lives and shaping their own future. The political dimension of this coherent set of beliefs derives from the 'democratic' nature of this epistemological position: knowledge is not 'truth' that is owned and handed down by experts, but a matter of perception and interpretation to which many can contribute.

This freedom to develop perceptions and interpretations which have knowledge status is logically consistent with the pattern of educational beliefs found among teachers who engage in practitioner research. These include a belief in the empowering purposes of education for all involved – students, teachers, leaders and the community – and a rejection of notions of schooling which prepare children for 'stations in life' determined for them by others. This standpoint is equally logically consistent with the rejection of managerialistic approaches to school leadership.

Practitioner researchers tend not to adopt unquestioningly something that someone else has labelled as 'best practice', unless there is ample empirical evidence to support that claim, and ample reason to suppose that the practice is transferable. Nor are practitioner researchers the kind of people who would expect others to adopt too readily the insights they gain from their own developmental work. While infrastructures to support debate and networking are entirely consistent with the ways in which practitioner researchers engage in dialogue, any tendency by official bodies to manage, approve, impose or regulate innovation and the transfer of ideas raises the risk of alienating the very teachers who would have most to contribute to a culture of reinvigorated professional leadership.

This chapter has drawn attention to some of the complexities and controversies surrounding the relationships between research and policy and practice. Adopting a position in relation to these is helpful for school-based researchers who want to argue that their research activity is worthy of the name and is worthwhile. It is also helpful for the leadership teams of research-engaged schools who want to clarify their expectations of the kinds of benefit they hope to derive from published research findings, and who want to guide staff on how to use such information as a supplement to their professional judgement.

Chapter 3

Evidence-based reform

The patterns and manner of research utilisation – its impact on policy and practice – were introduced in Chapter 2, but specific issues concerning 'evidence-based reform' merit further elaboration. For a school leadership team committed to making more and better use of published research findings, these issues present something of a minefield, which if not negotiated carefully could have the opposite effect to the sense of professional empowerment that research-engaged schools would usually be seeking.

Chapter 2 introduced four models of research utilisation: research to practice; problem-solving; interactive; and tactical. These have different directions of impetus in the relationships between researcher and user. The different pulls and dynamics within these models of research utilisation mainly reflect the different locations, remits, business needs and mindsets of actors at different points within the models: research producers, users and intermediary agents. It might be assumed that regardless of their different positions and agendas, actors at different points in the system, and others more generally who are keen to improve research utilisation, were fundamentally 'on the same side', sharing a common understanding of the aims and purposes of better knowledge transfer.

In fact this is not the case. Those wanting to increase research utilisation in education tend to fall into one or other of two distinct standpoints regardless of the role they occupy within the system:

- The approach and writings of one group imply that they believe that teaching is predominantly a technical activity, and that research can discover and develop the best ways to teach, and that teachers need to receive top-down instruction to implement those superior methods. These beliefs are implicitly, and sometimes explicitly, at the core of approaches described as 'evidence-based reform'.
- The other group consists of people who disagree with all three of those assumptions, believing that many aspects of education involve complex processes which depend on professional judgements and creativity, with much of the work and impetus for improvement coming from the bottom up.

A complication is that some proponents of evidence-based reform declare their support for both positions at the same time. This chapter explores the issues and problems surrounding the case for evidence-based reform.

One of the ways in which research influences policy and practice is through what was described in Chapter 2 as the 'research to practice' model of research utilisation. This is the classic form of research dissemination and knowledge transfer. At one time, and especially in relation to large-scale research projects, it was widely assumed to be the main – or even the only – way for research to have impact. In this model, the producer of the research, or an intermediary agent which has identified the research as important, promotes the implementation of the research findings. This is predominantly a one-way process, flowing from research to practice, although efficient disseminators will often engage potential users in ways that give the latter an impression of interactive partnership. As noted earlier, this model is a simplified form of one of Weiss's (1986) seven models of research utilisation. The adaptation of it developed here emphasises that the research may have practitioner as well as academic provenance, and that the role of an intermediary agent in the dissemination process may be significant.

In the context of schools and the education system, this form of research utilisation is associated with, and certainly most clearly seen in, top-down changes initiated by governments or their agents, and described by them as 'research-informed' or 'evidence-based' reforms. The Labour Government elected in the UK in 1997 described itself as committed to this approach. A major example of the policy put into practice was the Government's creation and implementation of the National Literacy Strategy, although it is informative to read the account by Moss and Huxford (2007) of the selective use of research within this strategy, especially in the field of research into phonics. Another example is the adoption and adaptation of aspects of the research of Black and Wiliam (1998) on formative assessment practice, although in a publication on its Assessment for Learning (AfL) Strategy (Department for Children, Schools and Families, 2008) the Government redefined 'Assessment for Learning' in a way that differs significantly from the researchers' original focus.

It might be expected that advocacy of research engagement by schools would correlate with a positive view of governments paying attention to research and using their influence to ensure that beneficial research findings are applied in practice. That is true to a large extent but not unreservedly so. The top-down imposition of 'evidence-based reform' may in some situations sit uneasily with the notions of research engagement by schools with which this book is concerned. Yet because the different approaches of 'evidence-based reform' (as advocated by academics rather than as practised by governments) and 'research-engaged schools' have similar intended outcomes and share much common ground, it is illuminating to explore the points of difference. These seem to reflect different views about the nature of teaching as an activity, about teachers' professional practice and how this evolves, and about the kind of 'knowledge' that teachers 'know' and the ways in which this can be spread and applied.

A critical perspective of evidence-based reform

One way of opening up these issues is by offering a critique of two representative writings from the evidence-based reform movement. The first is an article by Professor Robert Slavin, a respected and distinguished figure in the school effectiveness field and in the application of research to education policy and practice, with academic bases in the UK and at Johns Hopkins University, USA (Slavin, 2008).

Slavin argues that the problem in education is not a lack of knowledge about effective educational practice, so much as a widespread failure to apply that knowledge, i.e. a problem of behaviour. He compares this to failures to observe standards of hygiene in medicine, despite its importance being known.

Slavin considers that the new emphasis on evidence-based reform in education lags behind medicine, agriculture and engineering; that there must be 'proven programmes in every area'; that there must be user-friendly reviews of research identifying which practices are 'proven'; and that there must be government incentives for the adoption of proven programmes. Slavin also draws attention to the much lower incidence of experimental research in education in the UK than in the USA, and how this might be addressed, including through design competitions.

The strength of this argument, based as it is on the actual experience of education reforms in a range of contexts, and the clear aim of improvement, seems so sound that at one level it is almost above criticism. On the other hand, it represents standpoints of the 'school effectiveness' approach that are problematical for research engagement at school level.

Slavin's article treats education as comparable to scientific fields such as medicine, agriculture and engineering, and refers to 'proven programmes' in terms almost reminiscent of the 'Scientific Management' of F. W. Taylor (1856–1915) with its 'one right way'. While education is partly scientific, for example in its use of psychology, aspects of a teacher's work can also be compared to other occupational areas, such as the law, the church, the performing arts, journalism and politics – fields drawing upon case-by-case judgement and discretion, pastoral care, inspiration, interpretation and persuasion, rather than upon the application of science alone. (Actually the same is true of some of the work of doctors and nurses.) The point is that if education is only partly a 'science', then the idea of 'proven' practices and programmes can be only partly uncontested. Much of the basics of effective teaching, such as well-planned, interesting lessons, good classroom management, and so on, can certainly be accepted as 'proven practice', but Slavin is implying something different from that: specific innovations that have been developed and tested through formally structured experiments.

Slavin implies that these innovations will be the work of 'research and development organisations' and 'researchers, developers and entrepreneurs', i.e. work done by large specialised organisations external to schools and teachers. While it is only realistic to recognise that significant developments often require such approaches, the implication here, perhaps unintentionally, is to portray teachers as operatives who will be told by others what constitutes the 'right' practice and then will be incentivised to implement that practice. The reality for a teacher at the receiving end of an 'evidence-based policy initiative' in an average school is unlikely to be a sense of personally engaging with research findings and of reaching professional judgements about how best to apply them. It is much more likely to involve being told by an external change agent to implement a new method of working, by following government-produced materials.

School autonomy in using evidence

The idea of research engagement at school level rests upon a different set of assumptions. Its emphasis is not upon the top-down systemic application of 'proven practice', but rather upon the self-motivated professionalism of teachers, drawing from a range of internal and external sources of evidence to make judgements about what will 'work' best in their specific context. Research engagement ascribes value to small-scale practitioner research; generally, evidence-based reform does not. Research engagement assumes a proactive role for schools which take part in research projects conducted by other organisations on their premises, and a leading role for them in drawing upon, evaluating and applying published research findings to school issues.

Assuming that evidence-based policy initiatives will continue to come down through the system from time to time, it is worth considering the differences in the way in which they are likely to be received in a school which is research-engaged in comparison to a school which is not. For a school which is not research-engaged, the 'evidence-based' origins of the initiative are unlikely to distinguish it greatly from other externally driven changes. In a research-engaged school which scores highly on the Research Engaged School Health Check created by Handscomb and MacBeath (2003), two of the four criteria are that significant decisions are informed by research, and that people have access to tools that help them to challenge their practice. These qualities will enable school staff to be discerning about an externally driven, evidence-based initiative in three important respects.

First, they will be able to see a particular 'proven programme' within the wider context of the field of research of which it forms part. They will be able to have a view about the ways in which this initiative is different from – and allegedly better than – other related work, and to understand the points that are debated and contested within that field of study.

Second, they will understand the 'evidence base' sufficiently to see how far and how accurately the initiative is actually implementing that evidence. Some evidence-based initiatives remain truer than others to their underpinning research, as the following example illustrates:

> [Research found that] in effective schools, principals were particularly effective 'instructional leaders'...Where things went bad was in how these findings were interpreted and implemented. It led to much effort in the US to have principals acquire the attributes of effective instructional leaders. The problem was that this was done in a simplistic or superficial way...degenerating to...stipulations that principals should get out of their offices...to visit classrooms and supervise what was going on. This of course became unproductive or counter-productive to genuine instructional leadership since it did not embody very effective practice.
>
> (Selden, 1997: 248)

Third, staff in a research-engaged school may be better able to judge how the initiative can be implemented appropriately within their local context, and in particular, to differentiate between legitimate adaptations that would enable the findings of the underpinning research to be applied more authentically to the peculiarities of local conditions, and unhelpful adaptations that would be incompatible with those findings.

One product of the school effectiveness and evidence-based reform movements is the system of individual pupil assessment, target-setting and tracking used to monitor the progress of individual pupils that is now standard practice in English schools, at least in core subjects. In most schools, the gradual development and implementation of these arrangements, which were closely linked to accountability and inspection, were experienced as an externally imposed government initiative (welcome or unwelcome). Schools that are more inclined towards research engagement have looked beyond the mindset of compliance and seen greater potential in these data about children's progress to supply answers to their own questions and professional concerns.

A helpful new addition to the field is Bauer and Brazer (2012), writing in the context of the USA, specifically on research engagement as defined in this book, i.e. schools combining their own research with the use of published research in order to bring about school improvement. What makes this book interesting is that it is written from the standpoints of instructional leadership, evidence-based reform and school effectiveness, in marked contrast to the traditions of the school-based research movement in the UK. For school leaders content to work within those paradigms, Bauer and Brazer offer a coherent framework for school research engagement.

Balance between evidence and judgement

The second critique is of the booklet *Evidence Matters* by Morris (2009). Andrew Morris was the Director of the National Educational Research Forum (NERF) in England: a body established by David Blunkett in 1999 as part of the Labour Government's strategy to increase research utilisation. NERF was wound up in 2006: its final report noted its recommendation for the establishment of an evidence centre (Morris and Peckham, 2006), which was not implemented.

Morris (2009) displays the inconsistencies found within parts of the evidence-based practice movement. His case for the importance of 'evidence' rests, reasonably enough, on a very broad definition of evidence that includes performance data, inspection reports, observations of practice, reflections on experience and conversations with colleagues, as well as research evidence. He acknowledges (Morris, 2009: 12) that research has indirect influence on the wider forms of evidence. This position migrates into an argument that the kind of evidence needed, and lacking, is randomised controlled trials and other forms of experimental study, with a strong implication that this is the only kind of evidence that really counts, and that the implementation of the findings of such studies should direct teachers' pedagogic practice. Yet the examples of current good practice that he cites (Morris, 2009: 22, 23) are institutionally-based practitioner research projects, which represent the opposite end of the methodological spectrum from randomised controlled trials.

Morris shares the view of those many who have argued that governments should take more notice of research findings relevant to their policy concerns, noting (Morris, 2009: 12) that among the kinds of evidence that policy-makers have regard to, research evidence ranks well below other kinds of evidence. Morris cites as an example of research ignored by government, that 'the negative effects of excessive high-stakes summative assessment are repeatedly confirmed': effects of which many practitioners are aware through their professional and craft knowledge of teaching. Morris does not acknowledge the political reasons why the limited use of research by governments is unlikely to change (as rehearsed, for example, by Levin (2001)), nor does he acknowledge that issues such as high-stakes testing are indeed political matters as well as being academic and professional matters. Instead, his argument appears to visit the sins of governments (i.e. not taking enough account of research) on the profession, by wanting teachers to be even more subject to top-down prescription (i.e. prescription of 'proven methods').

Morris appears to underestimate the extent to which self-motivated professionals rely on the professional judgements that they have to make many times every day. He offers a future scenario in which a physics teacher, deciding whether to use electronic or manual data collection methods in a practical lesson:

> would have easy access to syntheses of research findings on the issue. If a relevant one were not available the teacher would turn to the professional association for advice. These associations would not only have access to and be familiar with syntheses of evidence on specific issues, but would be likely to be participants in review groups that initiate them.
>
> (Morris, 2009: 21)

Many might consider this a disproportionate investigation concerning a simple practical question that is more likely to be resolved through trying out each method as part of the normal craft skills of teaching. Apart from practical considerations, Chapter 2 summarised Hammersley's exposition of the theoretical difficulties in applying 'scientific methods' to the detailed day-to-day aspects of teaching (Hammersley, 2002).

Hammersley questioned whether greater direct application of research findings in teachers' work was automatically to be regarded as desirable. Is the application of research in a different context to that in which it was undertaken really likely to result in better education than the application of the teacher's professional judgement and experience? A further difficulty concerns how a vision of evidence-based practice like that of Morris, which seems to depend upon mechanistic prescriptions of educational methods, could be made to mesh with all of the checks and balances, discretions and responsibilities, embedded into the structures in England for every level of education governance and management. Some may want to question the point of spending time dreaming up research utilisation versions of Plato's Republic, in which 'Guardians' micro-manage teachers' work and the information they may access: a vision that is undesirable, unnecessary and, fortunately, unattainable within the UK's constitutional arrangements.

Power and control

These issues have a political dimension. The Stenhouse approach (encouraging teachers to be researchers) was widely interpreted as empowering practitioners to get into the driving seat of curriculum development and education reform. Governmental initiatives to address issues of quality, relevance and impact of all forms of educational research, including practitioner research, may be seen as taking control, by providing forms of official support that really have the effect of regulation. A polarisation along those lines does not entirely accord with the realities of the situation, in which both revolutionaries and regulators are found at every level of the system. The real polarisation is between different ideas about the extent to which teaching is a technical operation, amenable to mechanistic approaches.

The writings critiqued above pose a number of questions about power and control:

- Should the emphasis be on improving research utilisation within the system as it is currently structured?
- Or are 'constitutional' changes needed?
- Does practitioner access to, and use of, research require more regulation?
- Does the production of educational research need to be controlled more?
- Who decides, and who ought to decide, these matters?

The evidence-based reform movement embraces those who consider the 'evidence' powerful enough to speak for itself as the driver of change within current constitutional relations, and those who seek forms of imposition and control which would fundamentally alter the structure, legal position and nature of the teaching profession.

CUREE, the Centre for the Use of Research and Evidence in Education, established by Philippa Cordingley, developed a route map showing how teachers can access sources of information about research findings (CUREE, 2010). This was set out in the style of the iconic London Underground (subway metro) map, with different intersecting 'lines' for practitioner-friendly research summaries, exploring 'things that do and don't work', and tools and activities to involve colleagues in using research and evidence. These 'lines' called at a total of 45 'stations' of sources of support, some of which, such as the EPPI-Centre, are in themselves major and complex. Perhaps the barriers to greater research utilisation by teachers are not, after all, due so much to a shortage of accessible research syntheses, but rather to a shortage of time and incentive to access them.

Systematic reviews

A further question is whether 'more research utilisation' from the perspective of evidence-based reform really means 'more reliance on systematic reviews'.

Systematic reviews receive much emphasis in writings advocating evidence-based reform. They are portrayed as a particularly desirable medium through which practitioners should be encouraged to seek research 'solutions' to their practical problems. Like clean, purified drinking water, the processing and filtering of research through systematic reviews undertaken by trusted systematic reviewers makes it 'safe to drink'. There is a clear implication that practitioners should be discouraged from supping willy-nilly at sources of research they stumble across which have not been passed as suitable for their consumption. Systematic reviews have their benefits, as a quick way into a field; they also have their limitations. Usually these analyses of published research set strict criteria for selecting, from the thousands of relevant items published, those that will actually be included in the study. Often, only articles reporting empirical findings providing information which will fill all of a pre-determined set of cells will be used, which rules out not just material such as expert commentaries ('opinion pieces') but also the majority of reports of empirical investigations, because they will not provide information which exactly matches the chosen analytical template.

For example, in EPPI's review of research on interventions to meet the needs of gifted and talented students, systematic searches identified 20,947 studies for screening; of which only 101 were included in the mapping stage of the review. After the application of 'additional exclusion criteria' only 15 studies were selected for inclusion in the core of the analysis, none of which had taken place in the UK (Bailey *et al.*, 2008). This report is of little value to interested practitioners working in the UK: the filtering process has taken away the 'nourishment' as well as the 'impurities'.

There is also a more fundamental problem about research summaries which are written from the 'what works' school of thinking, with its preference towards positivism and managerialistic interventions. An article may be included in such a summary because it contains material that 'ticks the boxes' of a pre-determined analytical framework, yet what goes into those 'boxes' may not be the main point of the article. Its line of argument, its interpretations and its originality may all remain below the radar of that particular approach to research summarising. A research summary may offer one viewpoint on what a highly selective sample of research has to say on a particular topic, but that is not the same as giving an overview of a field.

Harsh Suri has argued for a broader range of approaches to the synthesising of research. She identified four possible standpoints: positivist synthesists, who would prioritise the reduction of any potential biases; interpretive synthesists, who would prioritise honouring representations of the participants in primary research studies; participatory synthesists, who would foreground the learning experiences of the synthesising process; and critical synthesists, who would pay attention to issues of power (Suri, 2008: 65). In the same study, Suri drew attention to the politics of publishing, because the synthesising process always starts from research that has been published. She notes that, for example, research that does not report marked differences between the sub-groups examined in a study is less likely to be published; and research that is at odds with the current prevailing beliefs or theories is less likely to be published (Suri, 2008: 68).

In a subsequent paper, Suri argued in favour of the practice of research synthesising reflecting the range and diversity of philosophical and theoretical orientations found in contemporary primary research, and proposed approaches that would achieve this (Suri, 2010). Suri and Clarke (2009) argued that:

Many systematic reviewers exclude a large proportion of research on the grounds of poor methodological quality using evaluation criteria that are biased against certain paradigmatic orientations...

The rhetorical effect of terms such as 'evidence-based practice', 'systematic reviews'...not only discredits any opposition but also has the political impact of favouring positivism.

(Suri and Clarke, 2009: 400)

Evidence-based practice in education and medicine

Further comment is appropriate on the issue of the similarities and differences between education and medicine with respect to the relationship between research and practice, because these are particularly relevant to the research to practice model of research utilisation.

David Hargreaves who, among his broad range of educational expertise, is a champion both of practitioner research by teachers and research engagement by schools, provided an insightful analysis of this matter, informed by a detailed investigation of medical education (Hargreaves, 1997). This was given as part of the proceedings of the NFER International Jubilee Conference in December 1996, and was, therefore, written at about the same time as his lecture to the Teacher Training Agency in 1996 on a similar theme which caused a certain amount of controversy, as discussed in Chapter 2. Hargreaves considered that the differences between these fields in their research to practice relationships were less than they were sometimes assumed to be. This was because clinical practice did not draw in a direct relationship upon natural sciences: its direct knowledge base was clinical craft knowledge, in much the same way that the direct knowledge base for the practice of teaching was craft knowledge of teaching. Beyond that similarity, the knowledge bases did, however, follow markedly different configurations. In medicine, clinical craft knowledge was fed in strong direct relationships from three sources: evidence-based clinical knowledge; clinical and medical science; and natural sciences. In education, craft knowledge of teaching was fed in a strong direct relationship by subject knowledge, and in a weak direct relationship by evidence-based knowledge of teaching. The evidence-based knowledge of teaching was fed in a strong direct relationship by educational research, which was in turn similarly fed by social sciences. There was, however, no direct link between social sciences and the craft knowledge of teaching, and only a weak direct link from educational research to the craft knowledge of teaching. Hargreaves concluded as follows:

> That one is fed by the natural sciences and one by the social sciences is not, I contend, the most notable or consequential difference from the point of view of research. Rather, I suggest that the differences that matter are that in medicine clinical researchers are also practitioners; researchers and practitioners are interested in the question 'What works in what circumstances of practice?'; and they are creating a body of evidence which contributes to the knowledge base that bears powerfully on clinical practice. By contrast, in education most researchers are not practitioners and there is a much weaker commitment among researchers to producing evidence about what works in what circumstances, so a relatively small effort is being devoted to this task.
>
> (Hargreaves, 1997: 231)

This comparison foregrounds the reasons for the weaker and less direct links between research and practice in education. A major reason that emerges is the different professional structures and career paths that apply in education, which may be more significant than the fact that medical practice is more 'scientific' than educational practice, and that the consequences of right or wrong treatments may be on a different scale.

Changing practices in research dissemination

The Preface included a description of a programme of research utilisation which followed the research to practice model, namely the author's implementation of the Epstein model of school, family and community partnerships. This was in the role of the intermediary agent, acting as the 'policy entrepreneur' to promote the implementation of some research which had been judged useful. Reflecting on the events related, it is important to remember that school leaders and practitioners have a natural resistance to externally suggested 'products' or 'solutions', and that political leaders and other stakeholders can find it irritating when people occupying influential posts use – some might say abuse – their position to push their pet ideas. Perhaps in any similar venture it might be advisable to use more collegial, subtle and patient tactics to encourage the perception that other stakeholders had themselves identified the problem and the solution. What this comment really highlights is an intrinsic problem in taking the 'agent' role in the research to practice model, since that will inevitably be perceived by some as championing a 'latest solution'. Courses of action which would soften that impression would also, in large part, involve shifting from the research to practice model of research utilisation to the problem-solving and interactive models.

That example of implementing Epstein's model of school, family and community partnerships incorporates some features that are atypical of research to practice projects in two important respects:

- First, its research base incorporates an accumulated mass of school-based implementation studies, many undertaken by practitioners, so it is not so much a case of applying theory to practice as applying research about practice to further practice.
- Second, the Epstein model is already a combination of a research and development project and a sophisticated infrastructure of dissemination and support, including user-friendly materials and a supportive website which has been thriving for more than ten years, going well beyond the average 'dissemination' arrangements attached to research projects.

The distinctive features of Epstein's research which made it easy to utilise in practice illustrate a more general diversification of research outputs since the main models of research utilisation were conceptualised in the 1980s.

Eric Hoyle, writing in 1985, identified emerging trends which he believed (correctly, as events have demonstrated) would change the research dissemination landscape (Hoyle, 1985). These included:

- the growing use of information and communication technology (ICT), greatly increasing the accessibility of research outputs
- changes in the prevailing epistemology, allowing greater challenge to the assumption that research outputs should be accepted as objective fact
- changes in professional development, which led to more teachers engaging in practitioner research
- the growth of the 'knowledge utilisation movement' – Hoyle's term for the development of intermediary agents specialising in brokering the interface between research outputs and users.

While the research to practice model tends to assume the dissemination of a large-scale academic research project, the outputs of the education research community show great variety. For example, in addition to basic or theoretical research, there are reports of applied research, researched evaluations of the effects of particular initiatives, and research reviews which bring together in a single report an overview of a particular research field. These forms of research are serving different purposes, and disseminating and utilising research in the latter three cases represents a different activity from the task of interpreting and applying the results of more purely academic research. For a practitioner or policy-maker wanting to clarify their ideas, a research review is a more digestible product than the report of a single research project, since it incorporates interpretation, comparison and contextualisation within itself, unless it suffers from the shortcomings of systematic reviews discussed earlier. Any generalisations one might be tempted to make about research to practice and evidence-based reform need to take account of this blending and overlap between the products of research and the products of knowledge utilisation activity.

Hoyle's 'knowledge utilisation movement' is accreted around some research projects to a significant extent. David Budge produced a case study of the impact of the research project on the deployment and impact of support staff (the DISS project) at the IOE (Budge, 2010). The research project had been funded by the Department for Children, Schools and Families (in England), and by the Welsh Assembly, and it had taken five years (2003–08). Budge describes the main methods used by the research team to promote their findings. These included many discussions with policy-makers, including through membership of expert working groups; the creation of a project website; press releases; presentations at research conferences; articles and other academic papers; and the development of in-service education and training programmes to help schools and local authorities to deploy classroom support staff more effectively (Budge, 2010). Budge analyses the impact of this activity, and concludes:

> There is, therefore, thanks to the Lamb Inquiry [Department for Children, Schools and Families, 2009], an unusually clear paper trail between the publication of the DISS report and government action in response to its findings. The speed of the response – just under six months – is also exceptional for a research study.
>
> (Budge, 2010: 4)

What is the likelihood that such a level of impact could have been achieved through the inclusion of this research in a systematic review? Clearly the rise in interest in systematic reviews takes nothing away from the importance of the impact of significant research findings that can be achieved through the direct actions of the research team.

Governments and research

It is not clear whether claims by governments to be engaging in evidence-informed policies have necessarily been helpful to the cause of evidence-based reform. Even to the most cursory glance it is apparent that governments pick and choose the policy areas to which they attach this claim, and within those, the nature and amount of evidence they take into consideration.

Whitty (2007) has charted this problematical relationship between research and policy over an extended period, and Levin (2001) has provided insights into the realities of political life that make this inevitable: inconvenient evidence is simply ignored. A review of the PISA (OECD Programme for International Student Assessment) 2000 study (Wilkins and MacBeath, 2002) suggested, among other things, that the effect of socio-economic status on attainment was reduced in European education systems which were fully comprehensive, and increased in systems in which school admissions policies operated to segregate socio-economic groups. The UK Government managed to find some parts of the PISA report to welcome as supporting its reforms, while ignoring the fact that the cohort of students studied in the report was largely untouched by those reforms, and also ignoring this evidence against its policy of increasing the differences between secondary schools. Husbands (2011), commenting on political responses to the 2009 PISA results, drew attention to the related problem of political eagerness to apply the lessons from 'successful' systems despite the difficulties of making cross-system comparisons.

This political selectivity in the use of research by governments will inevitably cause some to wonder whether, in some cases, a policy that was supposedly evidence-based was in fact selected normatively and then had attached to it some convenient evidence as additional justification for prescriptive intervention – and as ammunition to counter objections from the practitioner community. Such judgements would not fairly be made of some other national bodies. For example, the General Teaching Council for England made a commitment to basing its policy positions on research evidence, and scrutiny of its documentation suggests that this commitment was achieved to an impressive extent.

A more realistic question for governments than 'Are our policies evidence-based?' is 'Are our policies consistent with research evidence?', which accepts that the choice of policy is essentially political. This was the question that the UK Government put to distinguished experts in relation to its policies for 'personalised learning' and for its 'new relationship with schools' (Hopkins *et al.*, 2005). It does not do justice to these interesting essays to comment that these authors, while identifying a range of issues, did find a good measure of consistency between these policies and the research evidence. That might be, however, because both of these policies represented a political repackaging of principles that were already well established among educationists, so anything other than consistency with the evidence base would have been remarkable. The question that the Government asked on that occasion points towards another kind of research engagement, because in its general form ('Is this or that aspect of our policies/practices consistent with research evidence?') it is a question that might be asked by school leaders of their academic partners as a way of exploring the research–practice interface.

In this exploration of how schools can become research-engaged, and how schools might interact with the concepts of research to practice and evidence-based reform, it may be helpful to draw a distinction between evidence-based reform as claimed by governments on the one hand, and on the other hand as practised by universities and education research organisations, and to conclude by returning the focus to the latter.

The start of this chapter cited Black and Wiliam's (1998) work on Assessment for Learning and how this had been taken up and adapted by the Government. Recently, Dylan Wiliam led a research to practice project in a district of London, funded by a charitable foundation. This university-based initiative supported secondary schools in using Teacher Learning Communities to improve formative assessment practice, applying methods that have been developed and refined through research. This initiative was representative of evidence-based reform in providing a fair degree of prescription about how implementation should take place, based on accumulated evidence of the factors associated with effective implementation. That 'top-down' aspect makes it also a clear example of research to practice. The project was not imposed on schools, participation at school and group level being entirely voluntary. Although some groups took a while to become established, especially where senior leaders seemed to be giving little drive or support, the experience was that where teachers implemented the model as prescribed, they found it beneficial (Leahy and Wiliam, 2009). The twin factors of university leadership and voluntary participation meant that there had never been any question about the veracity of the research-driven nature of the project in the way that there can be with government policy initiatives.

This chapter has noted that there are tensions between the top-down nature of research to practice and evidence-based reform, and the more 'bottom-up' orientation usually associated with research-engaged schools. It is, however, important for schools striving to become research-engaged to have an adequate appreciation of the extent and dynamics of this top-down activity. In some schools, research-engaged teachers are almost entirely focused on their own internal, small-scale practitioner research projects, with insufficient contextualising within the broad field of education research. School leaders can choose ways to engage constructively with the evidence-based reform movement that will not conflict with their professional culture. For example, by identifying relevant issues to investigate in a range of ways, what might otherwise have been research utilisation in the research to practice mode, can simply by that proactivity be changed to the much more dynamic problem-solving and interactive modes.

This exploration of evidence-based policy and practice has also illustrated how blurred the boundaries are between scientific, professional and political agendas. Where does the 'scientific' role of champions of research utilisation fade into the roles of professional reformer and/or policy advocate?

Perhaps that happens at the point where the leap takes place from facts to values, or from research findings to preferred organisational arrangements for implementation. The first transition (to professional reformer) is represented by positions which take the form: 'the research findings are X, so teachers should change their practice in way Y'. The second transition (to policy advocate) is represented by positions which take the form: 'the research findings are X, so teachers should change their practice in way Y. So to make that happen, change Z is required to how the system is organised and managed.' The different agendas associated with school research engagement are picked up again in Chapter 8.

Chapter 4

Rationales for research engagement

Chapter 1 mentioned the way in which some school leaders see a strong link between their own educational beliefs and values, and their promotion of research engagement. The degree of connection between schools' espoused values and the actual behaviour of their senior management can, however, vary considerably. The same level of variation can be found in schools' professional cultures, for example in their general working atmospheres and the kinds of conversations that take place in their staff rooms. This chapter explores how some school leaders developed research engagement in their schools, by using four case studies of individuals who had themselves engaged in practitioner research and saw it as part of their leadership function to encourage others to do so as well. These individuals are presented and described in the round, not only because research engagement is brought about by individuals, but also because those individuals' interest in research cannot be separated from their strong standpoints on a range of related aspects of running a school. Chapter 6 looks more specifically at the systems and processes that leaders can use to support research engagement.

Individual teachers who become research-engaged at their own initiative most commonly do so because they are taking a higher degree that includes a research component. Other reasons are the influence of close colleagues who have become research-engaged, or because people in leadership positions, or the school as a whole, are moving towards research engagement.

Generally, when individual teachers become research-engaged it is the result of a specific stimulus: a requirement of a programme of study; a milestone or 'conversion experience' in their professional development; or the prompting of someone else. It is not particularly common for teachers to be research-engaged simply because they have always seen that as an essential aspect of being a teacher. This important point illustrates that teaching as a research-engaged profession is not the predominant mindset either in initial teacher education, or among rank-and-file practitioners, or in school leadership, or in education system leadership, or in school inspection. Those in schools who become research-engaged, or headteachers who are promoting research engagement within their school, talk about it in ways that clearly imply they see it as something different from the standard way of working. It is noteworthy that while some other professions, especially 'scientific' ones such as medicine, have a strong tradition of research engagement, the profession of education – which is actually centrally concerned with acquiring knowledge – does not. The comparisons and contrasts between education and medicine in respect of research engagement were raised in Chapters 2 and 3.

The literature of the research-engaged schools movement, reviewed in Chapter 1, suggests that schools becoming research-engaged (i.e. where research engagement is seen by some at least as an institutional policy rather than an individual choice) often do so because their leaders believe this helps them to achieve their primary purpose of educating their pupils and students. This perceived beneficial effect is multi-layered and complex. This chapter illustrates that complexity, by looking at the range of rationales that can motivate school leaders to promote research engagement.

The analysis shared here is a re-working of previous research published as Wilkins (2002), on the perceptions of eight school leaders who had personally undertaken practitioner research and saw it as an important influence on their approach to leadership. To begin, case studies of four of these school leaders are presented, which provide the clearest illustrations of a range of motivations and rationales. These examples are also related to the different models of research utilisation discussed in Chapter 2, but because they all involve a commitment to practitioner research, they are inevitably somewhat clustered. Each case study begins with information about the context, then describes what the school leader did, and also includes some 'authentic voice' quotations to convey that individual's own interpretation of their actions and motives. Later the other four individuals are introduced, in order to make some general comments about the characteristics of the group as a whole. The case studies do not fall into neat compartments, and there is much overlap between the motivations and rationales of the four individuals, but each has a distinctive overall feature, as follows:

- the first case study uses research to solve a problem
- the second uses research to model beliefs and values
- the third uses research to lead and develop staff
- the fourth uses research to promote teacher-led school development.

The first of these emphases concerns research engagement as problem-solving. At a direct level, research engagement can help a school to be more effective in tackling specific issues it is addressing, either by looking externally at published 'solutions' derived from research and development projects undertaken in supposedly similar circumstances, or by developing 'solutions' internally, through practitioner action research, refining practice through structured cycles of experimentation and reflection. Good action research will always take account of research findings from other sources, so this approach is additional to, rather than instead of, the externally focused approach. The relative preference given to externally and internally facing orientations in the search for 'solutions' will be influenced by the school's professional culture and the inclinations of its leaders, and by whether an external agent, such as a local authority school improvement service, is influencing the school's research engagement. It will also depend to some extent on the nature of the issue which is being addressed. If this happens to coincide with a topical matter in relation to which a government initiative is promoting certain 'research-informed' solutions, then the external focus will clearly be much stronger than where the issue is an isolated local matter.

Where the benefits sought from research engagement are of this direct nature, it will usually be a fairly straightforward matter for those involved to form judgements about the extent to which the benefits were actually achieved. These benefits flow from the application of research findings to specific issues. The following case study illustrates a school combining internal practitioner research with the application of published research findings, in order to address a specific issue that had been identified as a priority.

Jane: Using research to solve a problem

An example of practitioner research combined with the problem-solving, direct route model of research utilisation

Jane was the headteacher of an infant and nursery school. She did not encounter practitioner research until near the end of her career, when she and two members of her staff joined a local authority-sponsored research project, which provided the peer support of a research team, and external academic supervision.

Jane and her staff investigated the expectations of new parents about the education their children would receive in the nursery. Both the process and the findings had a profound impact on school practice. The research adopted the overall methodology of action research, so actual changes to practice were introduced step by step throughout the period of investigation, as well as subsequently.

Jane's research investigated parents' perceptions of the value of nursery education. Its purpose was to identify how to foster positive attitudes to schooling at the nursery stage, so as to bring longer-term benefits to the later phases of education. The research asked parents what they saw as the purposes of nursery education, shortly after their children had been admitted. This tended to produce answers based on the children's experience, so in later cycles of the research this data capture took place during a home visit in the half-term prior to admission. The method of investigation explored numerous specific issues and enabled analysis by various factors, such as whether the child had siblings and whether they had previously been to a playgroup.

A number of changes were made to school practice as a result of the research. The school upgraded the importance given to home visits and induction, and revised the information booklet to give more information about the educational content of the nursery programme. Teaching and support staff allocated more time to caring about the family unit rather than just the child, and a parent link teacher was appointed, to listen to parents and to advise on matters of welfare and on how parents could support teaching. The parent link teacher gave talks to parents about expectations for their children's education. An old, unused kitchen was renovated and converted into a location dedicated to working with parents.

These developments led the school to adopt the Epstein model of school, family and community partnership (Epstein *et al.*, 1997) (as one of the pilot schools in the project described in the example of research utilisation recounted in the Preface); and these outcomes all survived Jane's retirement and became embedded school practices. This was assisted by the fact that Jane had undertaken the research in collaboration with the staff, and in particular with the head of the nursery as co-researcher. Jane said:

> I feel strongly that home and school should work together for the best for the children. Families and their values should be respected, and the school should make every effort to individualise working together with families to take the number of different values into account. My colleague co-researcher and I held a number of meetings in the nursery and tried to make them very informal so that parents could freely give their views or ask for support. For some parents this worked; however, there were those who were not happy about being in the school environment for various reasons, who were difficult to reach. This was another factor that confirmed our conviction that the parent link teacher and the parents' centre were needed. Not only does the parent link teacher have the time to involve these families more, as it is part of her job description to do so, but also the parents' centre is not actually part of the school and we felt that many families would be happier there than actually in a formal part of the school.
>
> I had always felt that the parents were not as supportive as they could be; they wanted to be supportive but did not know how. That is why we decided to start at the beginning, when we first met them.

These comments make it clear that the focus for the research project was not chosen lightly, but reflected Jane's long-held educational beliefs about early years education and about the relationship between a school and its community:

> The information we found from the practitioner research was very useful, and was used by a number of people. I felt we should do more of this; teachers should have hard facts to justify what they are doing. My involvement in practitioner research came too near the end of my headship. Had I continued, it may have changed my approach. Had I been involved earlier in practitioner research, I would have been better at standing back, delegating more; a different style with reports back to the senior management team. I would have listened to people more, and adopted more of a partnership approach.

Jane's view of how her leadership practice might have been different had she become research-engaged at an earlier career stage is consistent with the perceptions of other school leaders who did become so engaged. Reflection, delegation, use of evidence, listening and partnership are qualities that are often associated with research-engaged school leaders.

Jane's research provides an example of practitioner research undertaken by a school leader having a clear impact on practice. Factors which appeared to support this impact were that the focus of the research was an issue of importance to the school, and that it was undertaken collaboratively so that it was 'owned' by the staff as a whole. Interestingly, Jane's research was the one project out of the case studies and vignettes featured in this book which did not aim to lead to accreditation for any of those involved, although it did draw upon external academic supervision. Later chapters raise the possibility that accreditation can become a distraction in some school-based research work, if the requirements of accreditation lead to high drop-out rates, and, for those who persevere, push into a lower level of priority the original practice-focused purposes of the programme. Chapter 7 comments further on the importance of appropriately chosen forms of accreditation, and external support for the quality, validity and dissemination of practitioners' work. Although they did not seek accreditation, Jane and her main co-researcher presented a paper at the sixth International Educational Management and Administration Research Conference of the British Educational Management and Administration Society, held at Robinson College, Cambridge, in March 2000, which in itself represented significant professional development for them and recognition of their work.

Some school leaders and practitioners believe, as a matter of principle, that it is right for them to model the values and behaviours they advocate to their pupils and students. These include promoting a love of learning for its own sake; the use of learning and investigation to address the issues and challenges of everyday living; and learning as a means to enable people to develop to their full potential.

Proponents of this thinking believe that the visible engagement of school staff in relevant research conveys a sense of integrity about how the school is attempting to live out its mission, which benefits its ethos and culture, and ultimately has a positive impact on learning. The nature of this impact may be less direct, and for that reason less easy to demonstrate, than where research is used to address a very specific problem. The second case study describes a school where the headteacher took this approach.

Edwin: Using research to model beliefs and values

An example of practitioner research combined with the problem-solving and interactive models of research utilisation

Edwin was the headteacher of an independent preparatory school (i.e. private, fee-paying – not a state school) for children aged from 2½ to 11, located in a county town in the East Midlands of England.

Edwin developed his interest in practitioner research through a research-based MEd degree programme. After arriving at his current school, he involved the whole school staff in research projects investigating the perceptions of the children, and the professional culture of the school. At the same time he introduced the Jackson model (Jackson, 2000) of separate organisational structures for maintenance management and for change management. These strategies were used to take forward school policies and to encourage all staff (including support staff) to be proactive in their own learning and development. He had also arranged for a university to provide an in-school certificate programme based on reflective practice, for an initial group of 15 staff (including some support staff).

Shortly after taking up his appointment as headteacher, Edwin also introduced pupil perception feedback as part of the working practice of the school. This formed one of a suite of strategies to develop the culture of the school. Over a period of two terms, staff were introduced to the concept and practice of pupil perception feedback; questionnaires were designed, trialled, discussed with parents and administered; then the results were discussed in a series of staff meetings. The brief comments below (a summary of the two-hour interview conducted with Edwin for this research) describe an individual personally very actively engaged with research, coming into a school as a new headteacher and establishing from the outset that research engagement is, henceforth, to be a non-negotiable aspect of the way the school is run. Edwin said:

Our school culture is linked with an evidence-based approach to school improvement, based on action research by individual staff and groups. Personal professional development is vital; this is now linked with our appraisal system. The introduction of our 'On Track' group including a focus on a futures perspective has helped a great deal: helping staff to appreciate that change is normal, that problems are our friends, and other Fullan 'rules' [Fullan, 1993], has created the right atmosphere to deal with change, also linked with the development of a language of discourse among staff.

Edwin went on to comment:

My view of leadership has evolved. Introducing the pupil feedback data has allowed me as headteacher to look both at my staff and at myself. It has provided the opportunity for me to experiment with and develop my views on how to attempt to maximise conditions for school improvement. I have learnt that the management of change is messy, and to empower you have to address the human side of the organisation. I appreciate more fully Fullan's view that a leader must start with a change in 'self'. I have become a more confident leader than I was, but in different ways. My role has to be as the person with most to learn. There is no conflict of interest between my research and leadership roles.

These two brief quotations contain a lot of information. The first conveys an impression that strong and effective professional leadership has been accompanied by managerial actions to 'make things happen', and that both are underpinned by Edwin's research engagement, which seems to have magnified his energy, authority and efficacy. The second shows evidence of reflection, and in common with other 'researcher-leaders', Edwin combines greater confidence with greater awareness of being a learner.

Edwin's practitioner research also impacted upon the practice in his school in tangible ways. As noted previously, Edwin's research involved two prongs: the capturing of pupils' perceptions; and the engagement of the whole school staff in analysing and developing the culture of the school. Edwin's approach involved an element of 'learning by doing'. He worked through processes with staff and pupils which were not only (nor even mainly) serving a research purpose, but which were actually implementing developments 'for real'. The results of the research were used to inform future policies and developments.

Another perceived benefit of research engagement is its developmental effect on the staff involved. This effect may include increased motivation, a sense of revitalisation, more conscious observation and reflection, greater confidence, a heightened sense of, and pride in, professional expertise, and an increase in constructive professional dialogue with colleagues. Professional development of this kind has a general benefit across the whole of a person's work and is not limited to the particular topic which is the subject of the research investigation. The following case study illustrates the work of a headteacher committed to this approach.

Sonia: Using research to lead and develop staff

An example of the tactical use of research

Sonia was an experienced secondary school headteacher, leading with certain innovative features the development of a new school that was to open shortly after the interview conducted with her for this research. She had personally used an action research approach since working as a young English teacher, and as a deputy headteacher had worked in a school where staff had been encouraged by the headteacher to undertake research projects. When Sonia became the headteacher of a very large community college (her previous school), she had introduced part-time secondments for staff to carry out research and development projects into issues that had been identified by a school development group. Some of these projects counted as modules towards MA degrees.

When she moved to her new post, which involved establishing a completely new school, Sonia took the decision that reflective practice and action research would be an important part of the professional culture of the school, and that all staff would be expected to work in that way: this was a factor in selecting staff for appointment. She said:

> At my previous school, I introduced secondments, for example a day per week for a term, or two days per week for a year. The staff development group identified the issues which needed to be addressed, and the time allocation they needed, and then invited proposals for research, like a job application. Then some did modules towards MAs, and some worked in pairs on projects. Five or six of these projects were undertaken every year for several years.

Commenting on the influence of practitioner research on her leadership, Sonia said:

> It is difficult to isolate the specific influence of practitioner research, but I think it has been fundamental. I believe that a more reflective teacher is a better teacher. My involvement in practitioner research has impacted hugely on my view of learning. It has made me realise how inadequate many of the conventional educational activities

are, in terms of stimulating and supporting learning. My role as a headteacher has focused much more on learning, and on working with individuals, both staff and students. The research has enabled me to put learning at the top of my agenda, where it should be. I have given more time to pedagogy than to the organisational issues. The leadership research has had a major impact, because it has made me question everything I do and my ways of working. It has made me face up to issues and discuss things through with colleagues, on a more personal as well as professional level.

I do not 'tell' because staff do not accept this any more. Nor am I good at 'selling'. I like sharing: I am a good listener. I have just met with all staff about curriculum plans, listening and encouraging them to say what they want to do, offering a blank sheet and coaxing ideas.

These comments convey an impression of very strong professional leadership, offering high challenge and support in areas such as pedagogy and curriculum, which are right at the heart of a school's purposes. Sonia and headteachers like her exercise very strong beneficial influence on their staff, despite, or perhaps because of, their insistence on high levels of 'distributed leadership', such as enabling staff to develop their ideas on a 'blank sheet'. This phenomenon suggests that leadership and authority are not finite quantities for distribution, so that if one person is given more, another must have less. Sonia's influence and standing with her staff, already high, kept on growing the more that she shared her formal authority through democratic and collegial methods of working.

Sometimes the champion of this approach to research engagement as a means to enrich the professional culture of the school may not be the headteacher. Indeed, sometimes such champions of research engagement who go on to become headteachers and holders of other senior leadership roles began using that approach at earlier career stages. The fourth case study describes the work of such an individual.

Andrew: Using research to champion teacher-led change

An example of the interactive model of research utilisation

Andrew was a senior teacher at a Catholic comprehensive school, who was in the process of moving on to take up a deputy headship elsewhere. As a young English teacher excited about the possibilities of what were then the new areas of media and communications studies, he had developed an interest in classroom-based research. Andrew was introduced more formally to action research through a school-based MA programme. After completing the programme, he went on to act as an in-school tutor for a group of teachers taking the same programme.

Andrew had recently completed doctoral research on the impact of teacher-led development work on teacher, student and school development, and he had also published on this subject. He said:

> My leadership role has grown alongside my involvement in practitioner research. I believe in teacher-led change and teacher capacity building. Through reflective practice, I have learned humility. Practitioner research means that I am interested in evidence. This is also a weakness; for example, I just ask questions rather than giving a lead. But this thoughtful approach may be more effective, because it gets people thinking. My role is informed by evidence. Plenty of people in my position do not interpret their role that way.

Andrew's practitioner research investigated how 'reflective action planning' (Frost, 1996) could be used to support teacher-led change in his school. This was essentially an action research project, learning through doing, which took place over an extended period of more than six years. The project involved forming a school-based group of teachers, who worked together as a team and engaged in individual, small-scale action research projects, which were accredited by a higher education institution.

As well as initiating this work and engaging in it himself, Andrew investigated and recorded the process over the whole life of the project. Over the period of six years, about 25 teachers gained accreditation through this programme, with a group of about ten being engaged at any one time. The scale of this activity meant that it had a significant effect upon the professional culture of the school.

Andrew's own involvement in developing, recording and analysing the process included the production of his own Master's and doctoral theses and various publications. At every stage, what Andrew learnt from the investigation was fed back into the ongoing development and improvement of the project. This immediate application of learning was one of the guiding principles upon which the whole project was built. This example illustrates the practical and philosophical objections raised in Chapter 2 to seeking to identify the impact of a practitioner's research separately from their impact as a practitioner who happens to use research as one of their methods of working.

The direct impact of Andrew's work was upon the teachers involved and upon the professional culture of the school. Had Andrew not been engaged in recording and analysing the whole process, it is difficult to imagine that the project could have been sustained in the way it was. The character of the project depended upon its leader providing a role model as a practitioner researcher, and the quality of the project depended upon the ongoing infusion into it of Andrew's findings. The development of the school's professional culture and the benefits to teaching and learning which flowed from this can, therefore, be reasonably claimed as the direct impacts of the practitioner research.

Andrew spoke of how his engagement in practitioner research had affected, or at the very least reinforced, his thinking and his approach to his role. This illustrates one of the indirect impacts of practitioner research: the research changes the researcher (or strengthens certain of their traits), which in turn has an impact upon their practice.

Andrew's case also illustrates the longer-term and less tangible impact that practitioner research may have. Shortly after the research interview, Andrew was leaving his school to take up a deputy headship elsewhere. In the research interview he shared his perceptions of the appointment process that had recently occurred. Andrew's perception was that his track record in promoting his particular approach to staff development had been a significant factor in his selection, and his new school wanted him to develop a similar project. That development could be regarded as one of the longer-term impacts of Andrew's practitioner research. Another, less tangible, impact has been the interest shown by other schools in the model developed at his previous school.

The case studies above illustrate the benefits that particular leaders may seek through their promotion of research engagement: benefits to problem-solving; to promoting normative values; and to fostering a developmental professional culture.

Four more case studies

It was noted earlier that the four case studies described above were from a research project involving eight case studies; the other four are briefly introduced below.

Colin was the headteacher of a large, successful Foundation comprehensive school, which had recently been designated as a Language College. His involvement with practitioner research only really started when, as an experienced headteacher, he embarked on a doctoral programme, which comprised three short research projects and one long one. He chose topics to investigate on the theme of headship, including an analysis of his own practice, which he used to improve his leadership practice, and to develop the professional culture of his school. Colin was active in promoting and supporting practitioner research in his own school, and in the school district, for example holding meetings for those engaged in similar work for networking and peer support. He used research interactively and with problem-solving and tactical motivations, primarily as a form of professional development for himself and staff.

Maria was deputy headteacher of a girls' Catholic comprehensive convent school with Beacon status. She first became involved in practitioner research in an earlier career phase, while taking an MEd degree programme, when she was working as the head of a large modern languages department in an independent convent school. She had also used action research approaches in the course of completing the National Professional Qualification for Headship. Maria was engaged in doctoral research on the effects of Beacon status on the school, focusing on school effectiveness and inter-school partnerships. She was also responsible for professional development within the school and used this opportunity to promote reflective practice. Maria's use of research was focused partly on gaining a deep understanding of the phenomena she observed, giving her work a greater flavour of 'pure' (rather than 'applied') research than is normally found in practitioner enquiry, but, nevertheless, displaying interactive and problem-solving characteristics. Professional development and teacher-led reform were significant motivations.

Humphrey was the headteacher of a large Foundation community college in East Anglia for students aged 11–18, which also provided adult and community education. He had a long-term interest in practitioner research. As a young head of a physics department, he had taken a Master's degree which was wholly research-based. Later, in a previous headship, he had set up an in-house management diploma course to encourage staff to examine their practice. In his current school, Humphrey had established an in-house MBA programme in partnership with a university. This programme included a substantial practitioner research project. Seventeen staff had passed through this programme, which was supported from school funds, and in which Humphrey took an active personal interest. He had recently completed his own doctoral research into the leadership issues associated with very large schools, and was applying the findings to his own (very large) school. His use of research was primarily problem-solving, and his support for research engagement was both as an expression of educational beliefs and as a means to the professional development of staff.

John was the recently retired headteacher of a secondary school in north-west England. John had first experienced practitioner research when he had been a headteacher for four years. He studied for a research-based Master's degree, investigating the views of parents, and how best to develop partnership between school and home. The findings of this research led to significant changes of practice and culture within John's school. During the middle and later years of his headship he encouraged staff to undertake practitioner research, providing release time and supporting staff access to appropriate university programmes. More recently, John had completed his own doctoral research on how headteachers change their approach to leadership over time. He used research interactively, and, at different periods, with emphases on problem-solving, professional development and exemplifying educational values.

Educational beliefs of this group

All eight of the case study participants presented beliefs about a selection of educational issues which appeared to be strikingly consistent. The only points that the participants had in common were their engagement in practitioner research and their experience of school leadership. They were of different ages and at different career stages, and worked in markedly different professional contexts spread across England. They gave their evidence in isolation. In these circumstances, the level of consistency of their views was notable.

All eight participants displayed beliefs in the empowering purposes of schooling within society, in teaching as a collegial and evidence-based profession, and in pupils as active and responsible partners in their own learning. They believed that their engagement in practitioner research had led them to adopt leadership styles which emphasised their role as learners, their reflective criticality and their preference for shared leadership.

Four of the participants (Sonia, Andrew, John and Humphrey) shared their vision for desirable future developments in the pattern of education.

For Sonia, developments in the educational use of ICT offered the potential of total flexibility of time and space, but to realise this it would be necessary to release schools from their custodial function, and to renegotiate the respective responsibilities of parents and educators for the education and care of children. Sonia envisaged individual learning programmes, using a competence-based rather than subject-based curriculum, with credit accumulation and flexible options. There would be no concept of school days or terms. The organisational implications of this vision were, of course, considerable, both for physical configuration and for staffing.

On physical configuration, Sonia said:

> There would be a small base, a local learning centre, one in every neighbourhood: children should not have far to travel, linked to a range of specialised facilities and sources of expertise. The young people would use e-learning at home, and for perhaps one day per week go to a specialised academy according to their aptitudes. There would be more real-life activities and vocational experience.

On staffing, Sonia commented:

The staff need to be generalists who are experts in the science of learning, who give individual mentoring for perhaps two hours per week. There would be a programme of lectures and activities, but no more classes of 30. Then there would be a network of experts in particular fields from the community and from specialised organisations.

John also wanted to move on from the custodial and institutionalised nature of schooling:

I would not create a school. We just need opportunities for people to come together for supported individual learning. The problems in schools are because of the nature of the institution: the school is there for the school, for its survival as an institution. Schools were created to keep children off the street. We need to enable parents and children to take more responsibility for education.

Andrew considered that 15-year-olds need not be 'bored by a disempowering curriculum':

We need neighbourhood schools with a much more flexible curriculum especially at Key Stage 4, with much more use of the community. There should be less obsessiveness about subjects, and valid programmes of study using different forms of accreditation. We need people with other skills, not just teachers. We should break up the Victorian groups of 30 children, and make schools a model of what we now know about learning.

Humphrey believed that every child's education should be built around an individual education plan, with the school offering a range of facilities and routes:

A key intention is to give schooling to the students, through the development, as an entitlement, of an individual learning plan for each student, negotiated and reviewed annually, and forming the heart of the educational process. The development of a curriculum that fulfils both statutory requirements and the need to individualise the learning for each student, involves embracing a high degree of flexible learning structures and supported self-study arrangements. It also requires the extensive use of ICT as an anywhere anytime learning tool and as a teaching and learning resource. The school will offer a range of facilities, and a triangular relationship between teacher, student and parent will enable the student to move through those opportunities in the best way. How to do this would be solved in discussion, by putting creative people together and giving them a high level of technical support.

It is now several years since these interviews were conducted (in 2001–02) and these thoughts were captured: a period in which much has been said and written about 'education futures'. Re-reading this material today (of which the extracts above are a small part), even against today's standards, it conveys an impression of visionary and enlightened educators. Perhaps one of the defining characteristics of visionary and enlightened educational thinking is that it transcends time and place.

The section above conveys a rounded picture of the individuals in this research, which has important implications, both practical and theoretical, for understanding research engagement in schools. These eight individuals were exceptional school leaders in many ways. Their involvement in practitioner research was one attribute among many, albeit the attribute that drew them into the study.

It cannot be overemphasised that this book does not claim any causal relationship, in either direction, between being an exceptional school leader and being involved in practitioner research. Nor does it even suggest a correlation, because clearly there exist plenty of exceptional school leaders who have had no significant involvement in practitioner research, and plenty of practitioner researchers who do not become exceptional school leaders. Investigating school research engagement in ways that assume it can be dealt with as a self-contained factor cannot proceed very far. In school contexts where research engagement flourishes, there will be other related factors present, emanating from the school's leadership or culture or history that cannot meaningfully be disaggregated or held constant for analytical purposes. In this field, local context and the qualities of individuals count greatly.

So, while advocating school research engagement, largely on normative grounds, this book avoids any hypothesis that would take the form: 'school research engagement leads to beneficial outcomes xyz'. Chapter 8 advances the less ambitious argument, again mainly on normative grounds, that research engagement may be an indicator of high-quality education.

Less-conducive contexts for practitioner research

Despite the potential benefits of practitioner research to educational leadership and change, the 'practitioner research community' in education remains a small sub-culture within the dominant cultures of school life. There are significant obstacles to engagement in practitioner research in schools, which limit the effective application of practitioner research to policy and practice. These obstacles relate to individuals, for example limitations of motivation, capacity and time, and to institutions, for example failures to encourage and support this form of professional development or to pay proper attention to its findings.

Many in schools would argue that the nature and pace of national educational reform in the UK, with its heavy emphasis on top-down managerial prescription, has done much to stifle creative problem-solving at practitioner level. This approach even characterises some official attempts to encourage practitioner research. Hextall and Mahoney (1998) critiqued the manner in which the (then) Teacher Training Agency implemented its laudable aim of promoting teaching as a research-based profession, which they argued was marred by somewhat mechanistic, limiting and disempowering conceptualisations of the work of teachers.

In order to counter these adversities, it is important to draw attention to the way in which the growth of practitioner research – and its increasing academic recognition – call for a reassessment of conventional understanding of the relationships between research, policy and practice, as was argued more fully in Chapter 2. Achieving a new appreciation of the potential influence of research on policy is a precondition for creating learning institutions in which leadership towards greater effectiveness is powered by research-based innovation.

Of course, these benefits can only be realised where the process of research engagement is undertaken successfully. Almost any school which is functioning normally will be research-engaged to some extent, but often this will happen through a set of unconscious and undeveloped processes and remains at a low level. It is also quite common to find research-engaged individuals or small groups of staff working within schools where the prevailing professional culture is merely tolerant, rather than supportive, of this approach. Progressing to the state where the school as a whole could be described as research-engaged requires a critical mass of the leadership team to develop a strong and lasting commitment to this way of working, combined with sound knowledge of how to change the professional culture of the school, and how to support specific aspects of research engagement.

These conditions will not be present in every school. Where they are absent, the scope for individuals to become actively research-engaged is likely to be limited, especially in respect of dialogue with colleagues and opportunities to implement findings. To illustrate this point, the following are two different cases of research-engaged practitioners encountering negative attitudes in their institution.

An experienced teacher was working in a middle management position in a comprehensive school. She had undertaken practitioner research in her school within the framework of an accredited programme, and she had gained an MA degree for the reports of her research projects. These were valued by the local authority (county) in which this teacher worked, and at the local authority's request she led a number of sessions of centrally organised continuing professional development (CPD), drawing upon these projects. She did not, however, feel able to tell her colleagues in the staff room that she had gained the MA, because she knew that she would be teased by her colleagues for being a 'swot'. Her achievements and skills had to be kept hidden. What does that say about the professional culture of the school?

Another school was one of a number taking part in the piloting of the Teachers' International Professional Development programme. A group of three staff from each school came together for some preparatory sessions, then undertook an international study visit together on the chosen theme, which happened to be inclusion. During the follow-up work it became apparent that at the school in question, the group of staff were not to be given any opportunity to report on the visit, neither to the senior management team, nor to a whole-staff meeting, nor to any other significant gathering. Considering that this was a pilot in which official bodies were requiring information about outcomes, the staff involved were surprised at the absence of even a token gesture towards taking an interest in what they had done. It would be nice to think that such negative and discouraging behaviour by school leaders was a rare exception, but information gained from numerous teachers undertaking professional development programmes suggests that this is not the case.

Research engagement which is unsupported and leads to abortive projects or flawed interpretation of findings can do more harm than good, including to the reputation of practitioner research. Even when the favourable conditions are present, schools need to choose the right moment to invest energy in the development of research engagement. Often there will be other aspects of change and development which should rightly be prioritised.

So, while considerable benefits can flow from research engagement, it is not an approach that could be recommended universally. In those schools where the conditions are favourable and used to good purpose, school leaders use a range of strategies to support the practice of research engagement. Chapter 5 explores how the practice and management of school-based practitioner research can support its quality, and Chapter 6 looks more specifically at the contribution of school leadership to school research engagement.

Chapter 5

Effective practitioner research

This chapter discusses some of the factors that affect the successful practice of school-based practitioner research, including ways to increase the credibility and usefulness of its outputs, and to manage the ethical issues it can raise. This embraces a bundle of separate topics, including quality, validity and ethics, each of which raises complex questions. These in turn are affected by issues regarding the kind of 'knowledge' that practitioner research produces. These questions suggest the possibility of a gap between discourse on these matters and actual practice: how might that be lessened?

The chapter's central argument is to draw attention to the interconnections between these topics. A practitioner research project which scores well on ethical considerations is more likely to score well on validity also, and vice versa. A project which is valid and ethical is more likely to exhibit high quality generally; and the amount of impact a study deserves to have is directly related to those factors. If it were not the case that these factors were linked together, it would have been possible to devote neat, discrete sections to ethics, quality, validity and impact. In fact, it is not easy to avoid a degree of cross-referencing between those topics: a 'to and fro' engagement that reflects the interconnection between these issues in real life.

The focus of this chapter is on improving the quality and effectiveness of practitioner research in schools. Chapter 6 looks at the role of school leadership and Chapter 7 comments on external and systemic support for research engagement by schools, including practitioner research. Chapter 5 is more concerned with the properties of the research itself. It is good for school systems and leadership teams to open up opportunities for practitioner research to be taken seriously, but those opportunities will lead to desired outcomes only if the research itself has appropriate characteristics.

Chapter 5 explores some of the factors that contribute to the quality and effectiveness of practitioner research. Here and there the sections include practical advice (which is summarised in Appendix 1), but the path to 'good' practitioner research is paved not with tips and checklists that will make everything clear, but rather with deep reflections which recognise complexities and generate doubt. It is progress to move from unawareness or unconscious assumptions to wrestling with issues, weighing competing factors, making judgements 'on balance', and being aware of risk and uncertainty.

Ethical issues in practitioner research

The British Educational Research Association (BERA) publishes guidance relevant to practitioner researchers, in particular its *Revised Ethical Guidelines for Educational Research* (BERA, 2004) and a series of short discussion pieces edited by David Bridges, including on professional ethics (Suissa, 2006) and on insider and outsider research (Bridges, 2006).

Venturing into the minefield of applying research ethics to practitioner contexts has been greatly assisted by the collection of writings edited by Campbell and Groundwater-Smith (2007). They observed that discussion of ethical issues in school-based practitioner research can be located within the context of other professions, such as legal practice, nursing and social care, which have also experienced the expansion of (predominantly qualitative) practitioner enquiry. There are ethical aspects regarding the relationship between field-based practitioners and their university-based tutors or supervisors; the publications that may flow from the enquiry; and whether pupils and students have given informed consent or are partners in the research. In applying the principles of research ethics to this type of work, it is not necessarily straightforward to delineate the activities that count as research – a theme that will keep arising in this exploration (Campbell and Groundwater-Smith, 2007: 2).

Cochran-Smith and Lytle (2007) explored the ethical issues arising from practitioner enquiry. They observed that these activities (see below for an elaboration of 'practitioner enquiry') raise a range of ethical dilemmas. These include how teachers talk about their context when they meet in enquiry communities; and, when the work is collaborative, who is entitled to write about whom, what can be disclosed and how that is negotiated, and who owns the data. The relationships involved in collaborative practitioner research are also problematical, for example where that 'collaboration' is nested within an accredited programme in which the university partner will also be assessing and grading the work (Cochran-Smith and Lytle, 2007: 36). A similar issue arises in in-school collaborations, where one of the 'partners' may be in a senior management position, responsible for the performance review of the other. In these relationships, there may be uncertainty about how much critique is permitted in the research process and who may critique whom.

Cochran-Smith and Lytle also raised the issue of how, when and whether to make public aspects of projects which reflect negatively on participants, and where this would leave the collaborative relationship (Cochran-Smith and Lytle, 2007: 38). This raises a fundamental question about the written outputs of the practitioner research movement, especially where these are produced collaboratively by practitioners and university partners. There are enormous pressures, both ethical and pragmatic, to produce reports which foreground the positive and which will reflect well on the partner school, and not to publish where the report would include findings that reflected badly on the school. With any kind of research, it is – or ought to be – the case that what gets published is the 'best' (in terms of the quality and significance of the research), but with collaborative school-based research the issue is slightly different. Here the question is whether the findings selected for publication are weighted towards those findings which reflect well on the school, with the effect that the picture of schools engaged in this work that is presented through publication is rosier than it would be if all such work were reported.

Inconveniently, perhaps, there are no clear 'rules' that can be applied to deal with the ethical dilemmas in practitioner research. As Cochran-Smith and Lytle conclude:

> *It is evident that there are many ethical contradictions, tensions and dilemmas that come with this territory and are not easily resolved or explained away. Even as we explore these issues…we are acutely conscious that the next task is not finding ways to fix or resolve these issues, but rather ways to think and talk about the ethics of practitioner enquiry differently and more openly, so that they continue to feed (not stymie) the work and support (not interfere with) the commitment of enquiry communities to interrogate even our most cherished assumptions and practices.*
>
> (Cochran-Smith and Lytle, 2007: 40)

Nicole Mockler (2007) reflected on several specific ethical dilemmas (including 'events' which overturned assurances a researcher had given to participants) that had arisen in relation to certain school-based practitioner research projects with which she had been involved, and how she could ethically report these for the purpose of discussing the issues. She saw the issues to be as much historical as ethical, concerning questions such as: Whose story gets told? Who has the right to tell it? Whose story is privileged above others and why? (Mockler, 2007: 91). A further issue was how much material should be omitted in order to protect anonymity, before the point was reached where this amounted to 'tampering with the evidence':

> *While these stories are the stories of my own experience, consent had not been sought from other key players, and had it been sought, given the purpose of the request, would probably not have been given by all involved. Whether that meant that in fact the reporting of my own experience would be unethical, I was unsure.*
>
> (Mockler, 2007: 91)

On the other hand, Mockler was also concerned about the ethical implications of not telling the stories, which would condone the ethically questionable practices that had occurred. More generally, she advocated that practitioner research should seek informed consent from all participants and should be transparent in its processes, collaborative in its nature, and transformative in its intent (Mockler, 2007: 95).

Nolan and Putten (2007) explored some of the ethical difficulties raised by action research, and the need to find solutions to these, as 'rich description and local knowledge will be lost' if action research projects cannot get through institutional review boards (Nolan and Putten, 2007: 404). School-based action research raises problems in the protection of confidentiality, because when the researcher reports their work and states their institutional affiliation, it is usually obvious that that is where they did the research. If it is a small institution, even where material is anonymised, it may be possible for people with local knowledge to identify individuals and groups referred to (Nolan and Putten, 2007).

Nolan and Putten also drew attention to difficulties concerning informed consent, pointing out that while schools and school districts may conduct quality assurance and evaluation as part of the culture of accountability, consent to that does not necessarily extend to research activities (Nolan and Putten, 2007: 403). They proposed some practical steps that might be taken to address the difficulties, including:

- involving teacher researchers on university ethics review boards
- minimising coercion in the collection of data, being clear that it is optional, and considering getting another member of staff to collect it
- bringing participants into decision-making as co-researchers
- building research activity into systems to emphasise its intentionality, for example issuing consent forms as part of the procedures at the start of a school year
- establishing school district/local authority ethics review boards
- making an ethics training course compulsory for teacher researchers
- working towards common documents on practitioner research ethics agreed between academic and professional groups.

These seven bullet points (a summary of Nolan and Putten's fuller argument) make good sense and hopefully ways may be found to take them forward. If that is to happen in the UK context, supporters and advisers of school research engagement outside the university sector, such as local authority advisers and headteachers in school networks, will need to make the running in developing the practice-located strands.

Boundaries and intentions in practitioner research

Just as the term 'home cooking' embraces a range of culinary experiences, it will be clear from previous chapters that the term 'practitioner research' is widely owned and has many meanings. In usage, the term 'practitioner research' overlaps with the related concepts of practitioner enquiry and reflective practice. Vagueness regarding whether and to what extent the 'research' can be separated from the 'practice' adds complexity to the issues explored in this chapter. This overlapping of concepts is both a blessing and a curse: the 'research' label is bewitching, drawing some reflective practitioners into mindsets and pathways which are problematical both for research ethics and for school development.

The central element in Stenhouse's definition of research ('systematic and sustained enquiry made public' (Stenhouse, 1983)) is 'enquiry', which can be unpacked along the dimensions of what, how and why. The 'what' and 'how' of practitioner research are difficult to disentangle from each other, and the 'why' can too easily be taken for granted. Chapter 6 proposes a range of motivations for engaging in practitioner research, from personal intellectual curiosity to implementing official school development plans. There is, however, a less positive aspect to motivations that needs to be acknowledged. There are some gaps between the picture of practitioner research which can be inferred from discourse and the way it can be practised in some situations.

It is important that a proposal by a practitioner for their school-based enquiry project should be subjected to critical probing, including from an ethical perspective. Almost always the proposal will concern a topical issue that the person has to address, and as a generality that would be recommended. A problem can arise with the choice of issue and with the motives for using research as the method by which it is to be addressed. On occasions there may be a need to advise that while practitioner research is indeed a very powerful and appropriate means to address issues with which a practitioner is working, it should not be used as a substitute for other necessary forms of action, or for a negative purpose.

Chapter 1, under the theme 'knowledge is power', pointed out the connection between engagement in practitioner research and the micropolitics and power dynamics of organisations. For example, one head of department had wanted to move curriculum development in a certain direction but had not won over their headteacher. They wanted to design a project 'to prove I was right'. Another practitioner in a middle management position had an issue about the contribution and commitment of one member of their team. They wanted to design a project, the findings of which 'would force that person to accept that they must change'. In both of these (real) cases the practitioner researchers were advised that this would be a misuse of research. Professional differences must be addressed through the normal working processes of the organisation: if that cannot be achieved, a unilaterally mounted 'research' attack is likely to make the problem worse. On the other hand, if normal working interactions could achieve sufficient rapprochement to enlist the 'other party' as a willing co-researcher in a jointly owned project, the research might contribute to some genuine problem-solving.

In these examples, the negative or confrontational intention was overt. In many other cases, it may take subtler form and may exist below the surface, perhaps below the surface of the practitioner's own self-knowledge. The practitioner research movement has always embraced a subversive agenda: changing the system from beneath and within, creating networks of like-minded change agents, like rabbit warrens beneath the surface of official structures. An agenda of practitioner empowerment and systemic reform through grass-roots improvements to practice is attractive, but those who support the 'movement' must do so responsibly. This means keeping a focus on addressing genuine educational issues in a collegial way, which will model to pupils a love of learning and its worthy application to problem-solving. The temptation to deploy research skills in the pursuit of personal and micro-political agendas is not, of course, limited to any particular sector. Headteachers implementing a practitioner research culture in their schools may in some cases welcome the additional forms of control this provides, and some academic researchers put a lot of energy into attacking their rivals.

Often, a proposal for a school-based practitioner research project forms part of the work for a higher degree. Much though the rise of practitioner research as a component of higher degrees is to be supported, on occasions the 'tail' of accreditation wags the 'dog' of practitioner enquiry. This happens because of short timescales, the need to produce data of certain kinds and quantities, the format of the report required, and the need to relate the enquiry to the subject focus of the course. Those requirements may not mesh well with the ways of working that are generated by a long-term commitment to the enquiry approach, an issue opened up further by David Frost (2007), as will be expanded on later in this chapter. Perhaps for some participants in higher degree programmes, obtaining the degree is the main motivation, and the school-based project is simply one more 'course requirement' to be satisfied. In some such cases one might harbour an unkind suspicion that a certain amount of creativity may be employed to dispatch this assignment, such as allowing the retrospective application of critical reflection to be read as if it were concurrent with the events reported, or representing a development taking place anyway as an action research project. So the 'why' of practitioner research is absolutely central to its ethics and value.

Turning next to the 'what' and 'how' of enquiry, we find out about things through reading, asking people, experimenting and observing. These are listed below in ascending order of importance for the ethical issues they raise.

Enquiry through reading

Reading is essential to enquiry in a professional context. The material may include official information and statistics, research reports and theoretical literature. Reading clarifies the question, and provides the language and conceptual frameworks within which the practitioner researcher will pursue their enquiry.

Enquiry through asking people

'Asking people' usually takes the form of in-depth interviews or questionnaire surveys. This form of data capture is easier to clear through ethical review than others, because the activity of data capture can be clearly delineated as separate from the normal work and is of short duration. There are still, of course, procedures that must be followed and factors that must be considered.

Enquiry through experimenting

The position becomes more complex when the enquiry involves experimenting, for example conducting cycles of action research, or setting up laboratory-style experimental situations. The latter is not as alien to education as it might appear: for example, different groups of students who are alike in other respects could be taught an athletic skill in PE using different techniques.

In the majority of cases, experimenting through action research or in other ways will overlap almost completely with the normal professional activities of teaching. This raises the problem of ensuring that the participants in the research (i.e. the students) have given voluntary informed consent, and that they had meaningful choice. If the experiment involves trying out a new method of teaching one of the modules of a GCSE course, what scope is there in practice for individual students to opt out of the experiment but not out of the course?

Enquiry through observing

More complex still is the ethical treatment of observation as a method of data capture. Yet this is a widely prevalent form of data capture in practitioner enquiry, often alongside other methods. This is not surprising, given the centrality of observation of pupils to the practice of teaching, and how much of it teachers have to do each day just to survive. Since teachers have a duty to observe their pupils all the time, it is by definition impossible to distinguish which acts of looking were specifically for the purposes of research, just as it is impossible meaningfully for a pupil to withhold their consent to being looked at by school staff when they are in school. Expressed thus, the point may seem ridiculous, but it is in fact treated very seriously by ethics committees, which will say that the rules for conducting research, especially involving children, cannot simply be waived because the researcher spends time with them in a non-research capacity.

The form of observation as a data capture method raises further problems. It may be naturalistic observation, or involve measurement against an instrument such as a lesson observation template. Or it may involve participant observation, which in schools almost always includes observation of the staff as a group (because a teacher cannot really 'participate' in being a student!). Participant observation is an established method of research. It may be overt or covert, with a preference for the former wherever possible. There are numerous situations where it has to be covert in order not to disrupt the normal behaviour of the subjects, and, away from education settings, to protect the physical safety of the researcher. It needs to be noted, however, that academic writing specifically about the ethics of school-based practitioner research tends to imply or state a ban on covert research.

The BERA guidelines are not absolute in banning covert research, which they refer to as 'deception':

> The securing of participants' voluntary informed consent, before research gets underway, is considered the norm for the conduct of research. Researchers must therefore avoid deception or subterfuge unless their research design specifically requires it to ensure that the appropriate data are collected or that the welfare of the researchers is not put in jeopardy. Decisions to use deception or subterfuge in research must be the subject of full deliberation and subsequent disclosure in reporting. The Association recommends that approval for this course of action should be obtained from a local or institutional ethics committee. In any event, if it is possible to do so, researchers must seek consent on a post-hoc basis in cases where it was not desirable to seek it before undertaking the research.
>
> (BERA, 2004: 6)

Academic research undertaken by practitioners

Part of the answer to the question 'What is practitioner research?' concerns its interface with practitioners' normal practice. Another part of the answer concerns its interface with academic research undertaken by practitioners. Much of the educational research in university faculties of education is academic research undertaken by practitioners, i.e. by people with substantial prior experience as teachers or headteachers, who bring those perspectives to their research designs. Many education practitioners working in schools undertake academic research in their spare time. They may be enrolled on MPhil or PhD programmes; they may be pursuing research into any of a wide range of aspects of education, using the same methods of data capture, analysis and interpretation as would be used by a researcher who is not a qualified teacher and not employed in educational practice.

The definition of 'practitioner research' does not equate to 'research undertaken by practitioners'. Practitioner research does not include the kind of activity described above, where an educational practitioner undertakes academic research. Academic research undertaken by practitioners does, however, fall very much within the definition of the research-engaged school. It is a worthwhile activity in its own right, and in some ways more likely than practitioner research to contribute to the school's research engagement more broadly, such as accessing and evaluating published research findings. When teachers find themselves drawn to researching, they should not be steered automatically to the assumption that this will be practitioner research (because 'that is what teachers do'): that would be as narrowing as the days when it was assumed that all research was academic. Teachers should have sufficient information to ask themselves, at any point on their research journey, whether their interests and career aspirations might in fact be better served by undertaking academic, rather than practitioner, research.

The defining characteristic of practitioner research concerns the range of techniques that are available for data capture, analysis and interpretation. The practitioner researcher has a wider range than a researcher who is not a practitioner. In addition to all of the techniques that can be used by an academic researcher, the practitioner researcher can use professional judgement as a valid technique. Suppose the research involves collecting data in the form 'the lessons I observed rated against the Ofsted scale of judgements as follows'. Or suppose it involves assessing the levels of special needs of particular children. Or it may involve looking at collections of children's work and making accurate assessments of the national curriculum level evidenced in each collection. In each case, only a practitioner who is professionally qualified to make those judgements authoritatively can do that research. An academic researcher would have to ask a different question and come at their evidence in a different way.

Widening the scope of practitioner research

The most likely image conjured up by the words 'school-based practitioner research' will be of individual practitioners investigating their own practice by undertaking small research projects, often as part of the requirement for completing a higher degree course. Probably the majority of practitioner research projects which have been undertaken up to the present time have been of that nature.

That same impression is conveyed by much of the 'methods' literature of school-based action research, such as Elliott (1985, 1991), McNiff (1988),

Halsall (1998), and Burton and Hartlett (2005), although all of these writers advocated communities of practice rather than isolated endeavours. Collaborative activity by a critical mass of school staff has been widely supported, for example by Middlewood *et al.* (1999), Frost *et al.* (2000), Frost and Durrant (2003), Durrant and Holden (2006) and by the National Research Engaged Schools Project (Sharp *et al.*, 2005). The progression of the practitioner research movement beyond small-scale individual projects makes it timely to emphasise the range of different scales on which practitioner research can be orchestrated, and the range of research methods available to school-based practitioner researchers. Figure 5.1 offers a tool to help schools or groups of partners to review the scope of their current practitioner research.

There are two purposes that might be served by supporting larger-scale practitioner research projects employing a wider range of methods:

- greater and more demonstrable impact on school development
- greater and more authoritative contribution to the field of educational research as a whole.

Scale
1. individual
2. in-school departmental team (or primary equivalent)
3. in-school cross-departmental team (or primary equivalent)
4. cross-school team
5. individual school with partner (e.g. higher education institution or local authority)
6. group of schools
7. group of schools with partner (e.g. higher education institution or local authority)
8. major national project

Research method
A. reflective practice
B. reading
C. participant observation
D. non-participant observation
E. ethnography
F. experiment
G. case studies
H. qualitative survey
I. quantitative survey

	1	2	3	4	5	6	7	8
A								
B								
C								
D								
E								
F								
G								
H								
I								

> Which cells in the table are populated in the current pattern of practitioner research activity? Tick any that apply.
>
> For enhanced quality and impact of practitioner research, which cells should be populated next? Tick any that apply.

Figure 5.1 Scope of practitioner research

The application of 'validity' to school-based practitioner investigations

Discussion about the validity of practitioner research has been nested within a wider debate, the 'paradigm wars' (Anderson and Herr, 1999), about the extent to which the products of practitioner research count as 'knowledge'. The mainstream academic community act as the arbiters of what can count as 'knowledge'. As practitioner research is the newcomer to the field, its champions have had to make their case.

Before exploring this issue, it may be helpful to recall, in Box 5.1, extracts from Holloway (1997) defining the key concepts of positivism, validity, reliability and reflexivity.

Box 5.1 Key concepts from Holloway (1997)

Positivism

Positivism is…based on the natural science model in which a belief in universal laws and law-like generalities can be found. One of the rules in this type of research is the quest for objectivity and neutrality so that distance can be preserved and personal biases avoided…Generalisability – possible application to other situations and cases – should be possible if random sampling is used.

Validity

Validity is…the everyday concept of truth. It is the extent to which an instrument measures what it is supposed to measure. In qualitative research it is the extent to which findings are true and accurate…the extent to which the researcher's findings accurately reflect the purpose of the study and represent reality.

Reliability

Reliability is the extent to which a technique or procedure will generate the same results regardless of how, when and where the research is carried out, or the extent to which the instrument is consistent…This consistency is difficult to achieve in qualitative research because the researcher is the main research instrument.

Reflexivity

Researchers are reflexive when they refer back and critically examine their own assumptions and actions through being 'self-conscious' and self-aware about their research process. This… includes reflection about their reaction to the people and events in the setting,…[and] on

---

> *their relationship with the participants. They also examine the way they feel while carrying out the research, and the effects of their observations on the people under study. [Reflexivity includes] the disclosure of [the researcher's] assumptions and biases.*

Most forms of conventional research observe, but do not interfere. Indeed, interference with the subject's behaviour would render the research invalid. While work of this kind is essential for theory-building, it raises problems for policy and practice, especially with studies that take place over an extended period. It is easy to imagine a conventionally designed research programme, examining an aspect of educational provision, which finds poor or mediocre practice, but has no means to interfere with it. The independent external researcher neutrally observes and records, and perhaps in two years' time reports their findings that the provision was, and continues to be, deficient. The researcher may have no remit to solve the problem or improve the practice, and indeed, the research might have to be aborted if others intervene to do so in ways that were not envisaged in the original research design. This would not apply, of course, where academic researchers undertake evaluations which are designed to include a formative element, allowing periodic milestones to learn from and apply emerging findings. The imagined example is of research undertaken primarily for academic purposes.

Practitioner researchers would not normally be happy to engage in research on such a basis, because of their overriding professional obligation to make the best provision they can for their clients (i.e. pupils and students). That means that if they discover, through enquiry, an aspect of their provision that could and should be improved, their first priority will be to do that. This is one of the reasons why action research is the preferred methodology for teachers' practitioner research. Action research aims to achieve improvement through intervention, so it is better suited to the needs of practitioners than research approaches which reject interventionary engagement between researcher and subject.

The word 'research' also has an ordinary, everyday meaning. Many occupations and industries engage in research as part of their standard operational practice. From advertising to journalism, from defence to cookery, from consumer protection to traffic management, the world runs on research. Education is no different: when 'research' is given its ordinary meaning, it is clear that teachers do it all the time, as they assess pupils, develop successful learning strategies and assemble curriculum content.

Among those many kinds of research, 'academic research' is one kind. This model of research tends to assume that the researcher is an outsider either 'spying' on their subjects, or overtly engaging them in activities which are additional to and different from their normal business – in both cases to serve the researcher's ends, rather than the subjects'. Under this mindset, if practitioner research is to be accepted as academic research, it would be necessary for the practitioner to step outside their normal role, and to step mentally into the academic domain and absorb its understanding of research. In that capacity, as 'honorary academic', they do their research as something separate from their practice, as if they were an outsider, observing the 'rules' of academic research. This approach does not get beyond an acceptance that practitioners can be academic researchers in their spare time; it does not amount to an acceptance that genuine practitioner research can also satisfy academic requirements.

If teaching and education leadership are to be promoted as research-based professions, this seems to require acceptance that research is an integral component of good professional practice. This means that a practitioner researcher is researching as part of their job. They do not step outside their role when they are researching. The research is not something different from or additional to their normal work; it is one of the means that professionals use to get on with the job they are paid to do. Under this conceptualisation, the ethical codes that apply to this kind of practitioner research in schools and local authorities have to include, and perhaps should be led by, the ethical codes that apply to normal professional practice by employees in schools and local authorities.

There is, of course, nothing to stop practitioners from engaging in practitioner research. The issue is how they can have their work accredited and how they can participate fully in professional debate through publication. Specifically, this includes what has to happen to enable reports of practitioner research to satisfy the requirements for the award of research degrees, and for publication in refereed journals.

Anderson and Herr (1999) moved forward the debate about how practitioner research can demonstrate rigour, by accepting that new criteria for validity are needed, which are designed for the particular circumstances of practitioner research (see below). Altheide and Johnson (1998) observed that the standpoint of positivism, which had dominated academic thinking, saw reliability as the route to validity: validity, as the accuracy and truthfulness of findings, was indicated by reference to reliability, as stability, consistency and repeatability of method, which enabled generalisation. In qualitative work, especially for example in ethnography, that relationship between validity and reliability does not apply. Instead, as Hammersley (1992) maintained, validity is found where an account accurately represents the phenomena it is intended to describe. Adler and Adler (1998) saw the relationship between validity and reliability reversed from the positivist position in relation to naturalistic qualitative work. Here, a negative correlation applied, in which high levels of reliability are achieved at the expense of validity. Validity arises from sensitive, in-depth understanding of phenomena (often people's views), while reliability arises from repeatability and standardisation of data capture methods, which reduce the likelihood of fully and accurately conveying the views of any particular individual.

Anderson and Herr (1999) advocated the promotion of new validity criteria that are more appropriate to insider practitioner investigation than the criteria conventionally applied to research in other traditions. Thus, 'outcome validity' measures the extent to which problems were actually resolved; 'process validity' assesses how the framing of problems facilitated learning; 'democratic validity' assesses collaboration and involvement of stakeholders; 'catalytic validity' assesses the reorientation and energising of participants; and 'dialogic validity' refers to peer review, including from within the practitioner community.

In promoting new validity criteria, Anderson and Herr follow Guba and Lincoln (1989), who preferred the terminology of 'authenticity' and 'trustworthiness' for work of this kind, in place of the terms 'validity' and 'reliability'. 'Authenticity' includes fairness to participants, while 'trustworthiness' includes elements of credibility, transferability, dependability and verifiability.

In school-based practitioner investigations, the issue of *external* validity may be speedily addressed, because usually such work takes the form of case studies which claim no generalisability beyond the contexts in which they take place. The insights and perceptions arising from a particular piece of practitioner investigation may, however, when considered alongside the outcomes of other such studies, and alongside the findings of other kinds of research, lead to the identification of new questions and lines of enquiry, and in this way contribute to the development of theory, a process described by Elliott and Doherty (2001) as 'naturalistic generalisation'.

How practitioner research contributes to knowledge

To develop the point above, and assuming that new validity criteria can demonstrate rigour in practitioner research, the question of whether and how practitioner research makes a genuine contribution to knowledge, and in particular whether individual contributions can be cumulative, can be taken further. Does the kind of knowledge produced through practitioner research go beyond solving local problems and contributing to professional development? Does it even get beyond reflexivity, to produce objective knowledge that has independent existence outside the researcher's mind?

This is partly a question of epistemology. Cochran-Smith and Lytle (1998) reviewed the debate about whether practitioner research produces a different kind of knowledge from academic research. They argued that most attempts to draw such a distinction look very much like attempts by those working within the dominant epistemologies and methodologies to marginalise the 'newcomer' (i.e. practitioner research) by defining it into an inferior status. These authors conclude that much depends on who is to make the judgement and what purposes the knowledge is supposed to serve. There is great diversity of output both from practitioner and academic research, much overlap between them, and, with one exception, no fundamental distinction between the kinds of knowledge they produce. The distinction is the one raised earlier: practitioner research outputs can include the application of relevant expert professional judgement in ways that academic research cannot.

If practitioner research is sufficiently keyed in to the conceptual frameworks of its field, and if 'knowledge' is a destination, then practitioner research offers a different pathway to what has to be conceived as a common destination. That destination itself may well have become more diverse and vibrant than in the days when there was only one road.

Discourse and the generation of meanings

Wilson and Wilson (1998) argued that an activity called 'research' should tell us something that we do not already know and would not have discovered in the course of normal experience. Good research produces results well above the level of common sense, and they subscribed to the view (debated in Chapter 3) that this could be like medical research, in which a body of knowledge is accumulated. 'Educational' research should be about learning – the mastery of knowledge – unlike research under the 'education' label, which might more accurately be described as sociological, economic or political.

In a separate paper, John Wilson (1998) elaborated the need to promote 'educational research' as an abstract concept with an idealised description, rather than merely describing the enterprise carried out under that label. One of the features of this concept of educational research would be the nature of the communication in which researchers engage with each other, which should involve the kind of mutual criticism that will make their thinking sophisticated and their research worthwhile. This activity may depend not so much upon theory or methodology as upon certain general qualities and ways of thinking. In Wilson's view, the concept of being a 'good educational researcher' may be similar in kind to the concept of being a 'good parent', where success in the role is not particularly linked to the application of theory or methodology. The activity is essentially interdisciplinary, in which a solid corpus of knowledge can only be built through deep and prolonged discussion (Wilson, 1998).

If knowledge is to build cumulatively, clarity is needed in how concepts are being used to describe phenomena. Bridges (1997) called for a more effective integration of philosophy of education into educational research, and also (Bridges, 1998) drew attention to the complexity of conceptual analysis in education, concerning the use of language and the meaning it conveys. His view was that in the field of education, it is impossible in practice to draw a line between the neutrally descriptive ('denotive') function of language, and its rhetorical and persuasive ('connotive') function. This makes it hard to give a meaning to a particular notion without simultaneously adopting a position on the underlying debates surrounding that notion.

These viewpoints highlight the dual purposes of discourse in research: discourse is both for developing understanding and for sharing and testing conclusions. It is, therefore, both a tool and a product of intellectual enquiry. That relationship is important in considering whether practitioner research amounts to more than reflexivity. In practitioner research, 'tool' discourse and 'product' discourse are more integrated, and may be difficult to distinguish. This means that the 'knowledge' represented in the language of findings may be of a similar kind to the 'knowledge' represented in the language of enquiry. There is no doubt that the champions of practitioner research, especially action research, such as McNiff (1988), saw it as both the product and the stimulus of more democratic and less positivistic views of knowledge. If 'knowledge' has somewhat less independent, external, objective reality than had traditionally been believed, then to that extent the things which practitioner researchers find out can be called 'knowledge'.

Newby (1997) argued for a mix of methods and a balanced approach to the issue of reflexivity. Reflexive self-awareness should also be developing in other research traditions, while at the same time, practitioner researchers should not be detached from traditions of thought which enable their work to be located within a broader perspective. While accepting that research findings cannot have the status of context-free truths, Newby argued that this need not mean adopting a view of knowledge which is no more than personal accounts of particular situations.

Practitioner researchers need to make use of conceptual frameworks which others can understand in a similar way, and which in most cases will be drawn from the literature of theoretical work arising from other research methodologies. Winter (1998) described action research as being about finding a voice with which to speak one's experience. This process, for practitioner research generally, will be greatly assisted if experiences are spoken about using the recognisable language of concepts and ideas which are already familiar to those listening. Practitioner researchers need to locate their activity on a wider map on which the landmarks and coordinates will be drawn from literature based on a wide variety of research methodologies. As they move through each cycle of action research, practitioner researchers draw from the literature of the relevant field in the following ways:

- conceptual frameworks with which to problematise issues, i.e. their rationale for issue identification
- understanding of appropriate interventions, i.e. rationale for choice of strategies through which to address the issue
- the terminology used to discuss the work

- tools for measuring and analysing the effects of their intervention
- the overall evaluation and choice of next steps.

The careful application of commonly accepted conceptual frameworks is also the key to the issue of whether practitioner research can be used comparatively: that is to say, whether insights gained in one project are of value to a practitioner working in a different – but apparently comparable – situation. This will depend on two main factors: what proportion of the outcome of the project concerns tangible phenomena other than the development of the researcher; and whether the descriptions of the phenomena offered by the researcher would have been subscribed to by an independent observer, had one been present. If an account of practitioner research is to have any prospect of wider usage, then it must contain sufficient information to enable potential users to make positive judgements about both of these factors. The example of action research that featured in the Tooley Report (Tooley and Darby, 1998), which was a paper by Chiswell (1995), was criticised by Tooley precisely because such positive judgements could not be made.

If that problem is to be overcome, it requires attention not just to the way in which the project is reported, but to how it is to be conducted throughout. The researcher needs to ask (and answer!) questions such as:

- Why should anyone believe that they would share my analysis of this situation?
- What evidence am I offering?
- Have I established a causal relationship between the changes I have made and the outcomes I am claiming?
- How can my readers be sure that I am using descriptive words in the same way that they would use them?

Where this rigour is applied, and where it is clear that the researcher has read the research literature relating to the problem they are addressing, so that they are competent to comment on it professionally, there is no reason why accounts of practitioner research cannot contain sufficient information to enable some valid comparative use of findings to be made. At the point where that occurs, it becomes undeniable that practitioner research can make a genuine contribution to knowledge.

Preventing the tail from wagging the dog

While advocating school-based practitioner research as a means of enriching professional practice, it is important to remember that the relationship goes that way round: the point of the research is to enrich the practice, rather than vice versa.

Earlier reference was made to situations in which the 'tail' of accreditation can wag the 'dog' of practitioner research of the kind that is integrated into normal professional practice. There is also a wider danger of research turning into a 'tail' that wags the 'dog' of the school's main educational purpose. This can occur in two ways:

- Practitioners can become so interested and involved in research that, despite its relevance and potential long-term benefit, and despite subscribing to the notion that the research is integral to (rather than additional to) the 'day job', it does in reality receive disproportionate attention at the expense of some other aspects of the role.
- The second way is a matter of mindset, arising from the difficulty of separating the activities of research and practice. In this situation, the practitioner applies the mindset of research to a wider span of their professional practice than is necessary or helpful: David Frost's insights on this (Frost, 2007) are cited later in this chapter.

If the 'tail' of research is allowed to wag the 'dog' of practice, one of the consequences is greatly to increase the difficulties of applying research ethics to situations in school that are at least as much 'practice' as they are 'research'. Research ethics clearly impinge on the way in which research-engaged practitioners carry out their practice. It is equally the case that the ethics of professional educational practice must also impinge on how school-based research is conducted. These two sets of ethical principles have to work in tandem; sometimes there are inconsistencies between them, but even where there is not, it will usually be right for senior managers in schools to keep the ethics of professional educational practice uppermost in their minds.

First, however, this activity of practitioner research should be contextualised among some of the other activities going on in education. Some senior practitioner researchers will be in a coaching relationship; some schools encourage a coaching culture in which this is the norm. In confidential session, the coachee will talk through their issues, which will often involve colleagues, staff and superiors. Only the coach will ever know what was said. The same person may belong to an action learning set. When it is their turn to take the floor, they share similar issues, trusting, as must the other members of the group, that none of it will be repeated. These are beneficial forms of development, which are not regarded as unethical. School staff who are practitioner researchers may sit on appointments panels where the qualities of members of staff may be discussed in confidential session. What distinguishes research from these situations is that the person's thoughts about other people are going to be written down and, in some form, 'made public'. It is important to note that the issue is the writing and reporting – having opinions about colleagues and sharing those orally in secret with 'authorised others' is an acceptable part of professional practice.

It is, of course, a different matter when those opinions are shared in unauthorised ways. Writing and reporting about one's colleagues in ways that raise concerns could involve a wider range of activities than research. Imagine a headteacher needing to manage a situation in which a teacher publishes short stories about life in schools, supposedly fictitious but including characters who are recognisably based on colleagues, against their wishes. Or the teacher may be in the habit of briefing a local newspaper in ways that cause upset. Or the headteacher may have received a complaint about comments the teacher made about colleagues in some public forum which have been fed back to those concerned. In these situations the issue will be dealt with as a matter of professional conduct and organisational discipline. Where a practitioner researcher, in the course of their research, causes irritation for acts of reportage which are seen as similar in kind to those other examples, probably most headteachers would want to deal with them first and foremost as breaches of professional conduct and organisational discipline. The fact that the actions are also breaches of research ethics would, perhaps, be seen as a corroborative but, nevertheless, secondary consideration. Given a headteacher's responsibility for running a school, that seems the correct prioritisation.

A further aid to maintaining a balanced perspective of research in the context of life in general is to draw attention to the extent to which observation and interpretation feature in normal living and have their expression in art and communication. Imagine a teacher, over an early breakfast, reading in the newspaper how an investigative journalist covertly joined the staff of a hotel and uncovered various malpractices, then reading the interpretation of yesterday's business in Parliament, and looking at the cartoons satirising recognisable people without their consent. On the bus to work, they might read one of Gervaise Phinn's novels based on his experiences as a teacher and school inspector in the Yorkshire Dales. In the course of the day's work, the classes they are with draw on Tennyson's poem *The Charge of the Light Brigade*, Graham Greene's *Journey Without Maps*, and Samuel Pepys's diary. Perhaps they have some ethical reservations about reading the latter, knowing that the subjects in it would not have given their consent to be so described. In a sixth form geography lesson, the students are using a summary of a research project on tourism, in which the researchers covertly observed the characteristics of tourists engaging with particular attractions, and the pattern of that engagement. For part of the evening, perhaps they relax, watching the film *The Queen*, depicting an interpretation of prominent living people. Finally, imagine this teacher settling down to write their reflective journal, in which they record privately their thoughts and interpretations of the school day. What do they call this activity? Is it diary keeping? Is it travel writing, or creative writing based on experience, or satire, or perhaps even poetry?

Is it investigative journalism? Perhaps it has the potential to be any of these things. But woe betide them if they call it 'practitioner research', because that may mean their interpretations are invalid, their conduct unethical, and their writing must be kept from the world!

Another way in which the 'tail' wags the 'dog' is when the mindset of academic research has too strong an influence over the design of practitioner research activities. The literature of teacher-led school improvement includes writings which explore the territory where practitioner research and the practitioner leadership of school development blend into each other. David Frost's concern (Frost, 2007) is that unless practitioner research incorporates sufficiently the methodology of action research, with its commitment to achieving outcomes through a series of cycles of experiment and reflection, the two activities of 'practitioner research' and 'teacher-led school improvement' could be in tension with each other. He argues that practitioner research can suffer from what he calls the 'QIFI' mindset: Question, Inquiry, Findings and Implementation. Frost argues that in this mindset, and especially where the practitioner research project is being undertaken as part of a higher degree, the practitioner researcher can take on (these are not Frost's words but a summary and interpretation) too much of the mindset of a detached external researcher. The researcher defines the question; investigates it by doing research 'on' or 'to' their colleagues; draws conclusions ('findings'); and presents these to senior management for 'implementation'. Frost draws in detail the contrast between that approach and the true spirit of teacher-led reform through action research, which is characterised by the continual ongoing interplay between gathering and using evidence, experimenting with practice, and managing change through collaboration.

Frost argues that the way to achieve beneficial impact on professional practice is the right combination of consultation with colleagues, reflection, reading, data-gathering, networking, joint planning, experimenting and staff development. By implication, these elements describe strong and enduring shared ownership and commitment, and very strong ongoing professional dialogue. Frost comes to the stark conclusion (for one who is such a champion of practitioner enquiry): 'This means that, rather than ask teachers and school leaders to become practitioner researchers we might do better to enable them to develop the skills of project management' (Frost, 2007: 181).

It is important not to take that statement out of its context; it does, however, come to the heart of this book's concern to marry the notions of research engagement and school development. For the purpose of explaining extremely important insights, Frost presents as dichotomies things which might, in the right circumstances, be found beneficially side by side. Across the whole range of activity of a research-engaged school, people might at any one time have needs for different kinds of knowledge for different purposes, and hence meet those needs in different ways. For example, a leadership team might be strongly committed to supporting collaborative teacher-led development as a general approach, while also from time to time commissioning internal research projects to meet specific institutional priorities – projects that might well display some 'QIFI' characteristics.

Concluding comment

This chapter has drawn attention to some of the issues for the ethics, quality and validity of school-based practitioner research. It will be evident that these issues are not straightforward and do not lend themselves to formulaic solutions. Practitioner researchers working in schools need to be conscious of these issues and complexities, but not to be paralysed by them.

Common-sense judgements have to be made about what is reasonable and appropriate in particular situations. In making those judgements, it is important to remember that the practitioner researcher's primary obligations are as a professional educator, working as part of a team, in the interests of their pupils and of the organisation that employs them. Remembering that the research should only ever be an aid to the achievement of those primary responsibilities serves the long-term interests of the practitioner research movement.

Chapter 6

School leadership for research engagement

Quite early in the life of the UK's National College for School Leadership (NCSL – its name was later changed to National College for the Leadership of Schools and Children's Services (NCLSCS)), its then Chief Executive, Heather du Quesnay, expressed the view (Hellawell, 2000) that NCSL would want to encourage headteachers to become researchers and to learn from study and reflection on their own and other people's practice: a view reiterated in the NCSL's official brochure (NCSL, 2001).

It is important to recognise that in educational settings, leadership is a function to which many contribute, rather than a role exercised by a single 'heroic' leader. It remains the case, nevertheless, that individuals in formally designated leadership roles, especially headteachers, have a major influence on organisational culture and hence on the extent to which research engagement will be helped or hindered.

The nature of school leadership

Talk of school leadership raises the question of what is meant by the 'leadership' of schools. From the extensive literature of school leadership, and from the actual daily work of 'school leaders', 'leadership' (however that is defined) can be seen to be exercised through a list of functions that might include the following: policy-making, governance, senior management, professional supervision, administration, and communication (external and internal). There are other words that could be used to describe aspects of the same range of functions. The point is that whatever definition of the distinctive essence of 'leadership' is adopted, it is through functions such as those listed that 'leaders' are able to do their 'leading'. Leading cannot be done in a vacuum: it requires communication through formal or informal meetings, or from a lectern, or in a think-piece or through administrative memoranda.

In the case of headteachers, they contribute to policy and governance through their work with their governing body, both in person and in how they manage the interfaces between the governing body, staff and stakeholders. They contribute to the other functions on a day-to-day basis. How are those functions and interactions used for the specific purposes of leadership, and even more specifically, for leadership of a kind that is conducive to research engagement?

Johnson (1996) explored the specific characteristics of *educational* leadership (by school district superintendents in the USA), and concluded that it was in essence a teaching process. This did not refer to teaching in a formal, didactic sense, but rather (by implication) to aspects of the best traditions of informal adult education, which are also the best traditions of professional development. These involve guiding, advising and supporting intelligent adults in a process of learning which enables them to explore the connections between new information and their accumulated experience. Many school leaders express resonance with the idea that the leadership of learning (not just for students but for the whole organisation) should feature strongly in the leadership of an educational organisation.

Fullan (1993) advocated creating an education system as a learning organisation, in which change is normal. This required teachers to be seen as agents of educational change and societal improvement, able to express their personal purpose. That is clearly more likely to be possible where leadership is directed to that aim. Fullan drew an explicit connection between this aim, and reflective practice and action research as tools.

The point was amplified in a search by Joyce *et al.* (1999) for structures which can guide school improvement through the growth of staff and students. In their view, these structures needed to transform the school into an enquiry-orientated, democratic community, committed to action research as a way of doing business.

Leadership and research engagement

The use of research by school leaders, or their encouragement of practitioner research as a strategic tool for school improvement, does not necessarily have to be associated with any particular model, approach or style of leadership.

This point can be made in relation to the familiar 'approaches' to leadership identified by Leithwood *et al.* (1999) from a study of journal articles: instructional, transformational, moral, participative, managerial and contingent approaches to leadership. Where instructional leadership is used, where does the leader's knowledge come from? This approach could be 'fed' by research engagement to develop and promulgate good practice. Where transformational leadership is used, the encouragement of research engagement might be one method of developing the commitment and capabilities of organisation members. Where moral leadership is used, the leader's normative values may include beliefs about education which attach high status to research engagement. Participative leadership might be used to foster reflective practice and practitioner research, by linking it to an emphasis on the role and influence of the peer group. Even in the case of managerial leadership, it is possible to ask: to what purposes are the functions, tasks and behaviours of staff directed? This approach could be used to support research engagement as a means of effecting change. Finally, contingent leadership, with its emphasis on problem-solving and the leader's 'knowing in action', could be supported by the leader's own research engagement. So, whether or not research engagement is encouraged does not need to be connected as a dependent variable to the adoption of any particular approach to leadership.

Another familiar conceptualisation of types of leadership is the analysis of leadership styles undertaken by the Hay McBer consultancy organisation (Goleman, 2000). The styles are: coercive, authoritative, affiliative, democratic, pacesetting and coaching styles of leadership. The analysis found that each style suits particular circumstances, and that each style impacts differentially on the factors that make up the 'climate' of the organisation: flexibility, responsibility, standards, rewards, clarity and commitment. It might be a struggle to make a case suggesting that either the coercive or pacesetting styles would be conducive to the promotion of research engagement by school staff, but it is plausible to suggest that good support for research engagement could be found in association with any of the other styles of leadership. So, support for research engagement is not a function of leadership 'style', either.

Much of the school leadership literature is mainly concerned with the institutional leadership of schools so that they function effectively as organisations, where effectiveness is measured by the achievement of 'outputs', usually in the form of student attainment. This conceptualisation of leadership, if traced back far enough, will find its sources in management sciences developed primarily in military and industrial contexts. There are other ways of thinking about 'leadership'. What do people mean when they talk about a 'leading architect', 'leading musician', 'leading writer', 'leading inventor' or 'leading thinker'? These concepts conjure up different ideas about what it is that distinguishes the leaders from the rest, and through what processes they exercise influence in their fields. Clearly in these examples, being an effective manager of a complex organisation is not a defining element within the concept of 'leadership'. Perhaps, as thinking about school leadership is taken forward, this might find room for the notion of a 'leading educator', and if so, it might be appropriate to draw understandings of that notion not just from military and industrial worlds, but also perhaps from the worlds of creativity and ideas.

In leadership development work, a distinction can sometimes be drawn between 'leading how' and 'leading where'. Much officially sponsored leadership development for headteachers in England seems to be concerned with 'leading how': that is to say, the processes of leadership which will deliver the best 'returns' in a situation where the shape and purpose of the organisation, and its success criteria, are externally imposed and must be taken as fixed and given. This kind of leadership requires keenness, loyalty and resourcefulness to make marginal adjustments to the inherited status quo, so as to deliver required short-term outputs. Thus expressed, that describes a manager rather than a leader. For many headteachers in England working within highly prescriptive expectations that is a more accurate description of how they spend most of each day.

For similar reasons, people working in countries with highly centralised or heavily bureaucratic education systems can find it difficult to relate to the emphasis on 'leadership' in the school improvement literature of English-speaking developed countries, because the functions that their school principals are paid to perform are more accurately described as 'educational administration' – a term used generally in the UK until the early 1980s. 'Leadership' requires attention to the 'where?' as well as to the 'how?'. Leaders are those whose ideas will shape the system of the future, who will help to conceive the educational aims and infrastructures that will be fit for purpose in the longer term, and who have the capability to enable and sustain long-term processes of fundamental change.

The system needs both leadership and management, and almost all 'school leaders' combine both functions. The following considerations on how school leaders support research engagement have regard to visionary leading educators who are also effective managers and administrators. The individuals introduced in the case studies in Chapter 4, who will be referred to again in this chapter, exemplified those qualities.

'Researcher-leaders'

The term 'researcher-leaders' might be applied to school leaders with significant personal experience of practitioner research and research engagement generally. What characteristics might they be expected to display? A process of rational argument proceeds, by deduction, to an expectation that school leaders who engage in, and have an affinity for, practitioner research *ought* to be likely to exhibit certain characteristics in their approach to leadership. At the most basic level, they can be expected to understand the concepts of practitioner research and reflective practice, rather than being bemused by them. They ought to want the culture of their school to encourage such work, rather than to sneer dismissively at it, and so on. In this way, a deductive process underpinned by scholarship leads to the formulation of a set of expectations.

To test these expectations, a group was formed (through a conference on practitioner research) of middle managers in secondary schools who had personal experience of undertaking practitioner research, and who were working in institutions broadly representative of the generality of secondary schools, i.e. schools not distinguished as being particularly supportive of practitioner research. A questionnaire sought their reactions to a list of 34 positive attributes that might, on rational grounds, be associated with a school leader committed to supporting practitioner research. The questionnaire also included three sections of open questions inviting comments on factors helping and hindering practitioner research in schools, issues regarding the use of published research findings, and questions about the then current Best Practice Research Scholarship scheme. The responses to this survey helped to identify the most significant attributes that might be expected of a school leader committed to supporting practitioner research.

To connect this work to its theoretical field, modifications and developments were made to a model of leadership support for action learning that had been proposed by Yuen and Cheng (2000), in order to produce a checklist for reviewing leaders' support for practitioner research. The classification of factors into the three groups of *inspiring, social supporting* and *enabling* are drawn directly from Yuen and Cheng's model. The questions under these headings were derived from the research with the middle managers described above. The checklist, in a revised form, is set out below.

Box 6.1 Checklist for reviewing leaders' support for practitioner research

A. Inspiring

1. How and to what extent does the leadership team build and institutionalise a shared vision which is consistent with encouraging practitioner research?
2. How and to what extent does the leadership team encourage staff to develop their roles in ways which are conducive to practitioner research?
3. How and to what extent does the leadership team ensure that senior managers give support to staff who are engaged in practitioner research, and take interest in, and value, their findings?

B. Social supporting

4. How and to what extent does the leadership team prioritise professional development in overall school development, giving it adequate resources, in ways which foster practitioner research?
5. How and to what extent does the leadership team ensure that practitioner research undertaken by staff is relevant to the interests and needs of other staff?
6. How and to what extent does the leadership team encourage staff to work collaboratively?

C. Enabling

7. How and to what extent does the leadership team provide intellectual stimulation by drawing upon professional reading and published research findings?

---

8. How and to what extent does the leadership team ensure that staff are given time to engage in practitioner research?
9. How and to what extent does the leadership team ensure that staff are given time and opportunity to disseminate their practitioner research?
10. How and to what extent does the leadership team enable staff engaged in practitioner research to develop their skills in sharing their results with colleagues?
11. How and to what extent does the leadership team procure external support, e.g. from a university, for staff engaged in practitioner research?

Schools in the UK have a high level of self-governance, and within schools, headteachers have great authority over the working lives and careers of their staff. National government has greatly increased its control of schools, including through the use of performance data and the linking of funding to specific initiatives which give schools strong incentives to comply with a suite of policies even though they are not legally required to do so. That tendency notwithstanding, one of the few areas in which headteachers continue to have considerable freedom is in how they choose to develop the professional culture of their school, and how to approach their own continuing professional development. Each of the 11 questions in the checklist above concerns a matter over which headteachers retain extensive discretion. Perhaps that is why schools, which have been on a convergent trajectory in relation to some aspects of their work, remain so varied in their stances towards research engagement.

Developmental stages of researcher-leadership

The checklist above was used as one of the analytical lenses to examine the material gained through the eight case studies conducted with the individuals introduced in the case studies in Chapter 4. From that analysis, a series of developmental stages were identified through which a 'researcher-leader' might progress, as set out below.

Stage one: Personal journey

At this stage, the leader's engagement in practitioner research is predominantly a personal (i.e. individual) activity, which stimulates reflection on the approach taken by the individual to performing their own role.

Stage two: Change agent

In addition to meeting the characteristics of stage one, the leader is actively using ideas and insights stimulated by their own engagement in practitioner research to bring about change in their organisation, including through the managerial exercise of authority, as well as overt professional leadership.

Stage three: Culture of practitioner research is significantly institutionalised

In addition to meeting the characteristics of stage two, the leader has established active support and ownership by the senior leadership team for the culture of practitioner research, and a number of staff are engaged in practitioner research with the institution's encouragement and support.

Stage four: Culture of practitioner research is fully institutionalised

In addition to meeting the characteristics of stage three, the leader has established the culture of practitioner research as a central and non-negotiable feature of how the organisation goes about its business.

To complete the story it is interesting, but perhaps not surprising, that of the eight participants in that study, the three clearly demonstrating stage four characteristics were the three experienced headteachers in their second and third headships and still with a good period of their career ahead of them (Sonia, Edwin and Humphrey). The rest were at, or bordering on, stage three. In two cases (Jane and John), retirement had limited further progression. Two others (Maria and Andrew) were not headteachers and could not realistically have reached a higher stage from their current positions.

How some researcher-leaders manage staff

Johnston and Caldwell (2001) considered that the leadership of schools as learning organisations was supported by, among other factors, inclusive collaborative structures and learning-focused leadership. The latter involved the leader in providing a positive role model of professional learning, with an emphasis on co-learning, flexibility of roles between team leader and team member, and opportunities for individuals and groups to assume multiple roles (Johnston and Caldwell, 2001). In modern practice this may include promoting and supporting professional learning communities (Stoll and Seashore Louis, 2007).

The researcher-leaders introduced in Chapter 4 offered a range of perceptions about their management and leadership styles and about the culture of their organisations. The most developed model was provided by Edwin, the headteacher of an independent preparatory school. Edwin had started involving the school staff in considering the culture of the school at his own appointment interview, and this had continued into a major whole-school research study over a period of months. This had culminated in an increased degree of consensus and greater clarity about the culture of the school. Edwin promoted the notions of a learning school, capturing and responding to the pupils' voice, and the professional development of staff. He had introduced the management structure developed by Jackson (2000), which comprised separate teams for 'maintenance' management and for the leadership of change, with some overlapping membership. One of the principles of the latter team, termed the 'On Track' group, was that 'rank was left at the door'; for example, a member of the support staff emerged in a leadership role for part of the work of this group. Edwin described his style as 'learning focused, highly reflective, and evidence-based': 'my role has to be the person with most to learn'. He minimised management team meetings, preferring to share news and discussion with the whole staff. Edwin, like other participants in this research, exemplified the leadership framework advocated by Yuen and Cheng (2000) for facilitating teachers' action learning.

Sonia also emphasised the role of headteacher as 'head learner', and while the culture of her previous school had been 'democratic, participative and creative', she wished to take this further in her current, newly developing school 'to a less formal but more truly participative process of decision-making...with leadership opportunities for all'.

Inclusive and collaborative approaches to decision-making were also evident in comments by other participants:

> My style was a partnership approach, encouraging trust and sharing; a stable and experienced staff enabled us to achieve a culture which shared strengths and concerns.
>
> (Jane)

> There is a dynamic within the school culture which is moving the school towards greater transparency and more inclusive decision-making.
>
> (Maria)

> The power to act effectively is not governed by role. I have a healthy disrespect for status but I respect vision. I attach importance to a consensus of view. I ask questions and get people thinking.
>
> (Andrew)

> I now manage the senior management team differently. I no longer chair meetings. I insist on a structured approach. The chair rotates by terms and then by items. Others can put their own papers to meetings which are planned in advance: we have two hours and we interact with the information. My management style includes the notion of all staff having the maximum information and openness.
>
> (Colin)

I practise much delegation. My approach is evidence-based. I read, listen and share with others. There is high collegiality in the staffroom: I aim for dispersed leadership and a blame-free, educative environment.

(Humphrey)

Some participants referred to diversity within the organisational culture:

There is more than one culture in the school, and we inhabit several cultures at once.

(Andrew)

I am capable of leading the school forward at a more rapid rate of improvement, and compromise more than I would like in order to maintain a sense of ownership by the more traditional elements within the institution. I see myself as a bridge between the tensions within the organisation. There is still a rearguard action from older staff who do not value the views of younger staff. For these reasons the school is an evolutionary organisation rather than a radical innovator: we are here for the long run of constant review and self-improvement.

(Colin)

All organisations depend for their survival on means of surveillance and control of the activities of their members. The combined effects of school autonomy, increased accountability and performance management regimes has been to strengthen the hierarchical nature of schools and to widen their internal power differentials. The participants' stances on this were interesting. All refuted, with justification, any suggestion of authoritarianism, and all stressed their use of delegation, teamwork, a consultative and sharing approach, and modelling listening and learning. On the other hand, they were overt about their own determination of the big issues of strategy and philosophy:

The statement of strategic intent came from me. I wrote it.

(Humphrey)

Leadership is vital. I show some direction and bring external information and judgement. I take the decisions on personnel matters.

(Colin)

My leadership style is based on an enthusiasm for learning as our core business. I am passionate about learning: people cannot be good teachers unless they are good learners. I practise what I preach, so I cannot be authoritarian or dogmatic; it forces me to a collaborative and democratic way of working. I work with people, I manage their enthusiasm and interest, I get them to feel so committed and passionate that they go beyond the call of duty.

(Sonia)

These perceptions help to map the actual scope of delegated decision-making within contexts where the non-negotiables of organisational culture have been clearly established. Sonia's curriculum leaders, responding to their 'blank sheet' (see Chapter 4) did so in the context of having joined the organisation knowing its aims and approach, and having been carefully selected and inducted as a team. The 'blank sheet' was the collective property of the new organisation: Sonia used the term 'collective brain' of her previous school.

Some of the participants acknowledged almost apologetically the strength of their impact as leaders. Sonia said that one of her early and very influential role models had been described as 'Machiavellian', because she had planted the seeds of ideas and allowed people to believe they were their own. Other participants said:

Someone felt I was 'manipulative', but they meant it as a compliment, that I was acting in the school's interests: consulting but with clear goals in mind.

(Edwin)

I adopt a very thoughtful approach, which may not be what people want, but it may be more effective because it forces people to think.

(Andrew)

Consulting individual members of staff on the key issues of teaching and learning, insisting on meaningful dialogue, and listening in ways which force staff to articulate their professional judgements, represent more powerful tools for securing their engagement and acceptance of shared responsibility than traditional authoritarian methods. The latter were usually associated with sub-cultures within which staff could establish distance from (or opposition to) 'management's view', or adopt survival tactics, such as 'I keep my opinions to myself and just fulfil my contract'. Intensive listening in the context of an open and trusting culture is also an effective source of information and feedback.

The increased availability of data about individual pupil attainment, increased use of lesson observation, and increased use of school ICT systems for lesson plans and teaching resources have led to intensification of the surveillance of teachers' work:

We are providing the support to enable teaching staff to get back to focusing on teaching and learning, but this threatens their comfort zone because other activities are easier than teaching and learning.

(Humphrey)

From September, I will no longer teach. I will use that time to spend longer on lesson observation and meeting groups of pupils to look at their work.

(Colin)

These techniques of engagement, information-sharing, team development and observation are becoming the most effective strategies for exercising surveillance and control in schools. It is essential to have regard to the purposes to which these techniques are directed. In all of the cases in the research reported, leaders used their influence to promote educational values in educative ways, with the aim of maximising learning for everyone. This has to be distinguished from reprehensible uses of power.

The psychological and moral bases of school leadership are rising in significance. For staff, this raises the importance of the nature of their involvement with, and commitment to, the organisation, and their ability to fit in with its culture. For school leaders, cultivating research engagement may be a powerful means of enriching the school's professional culture, but it is not a venture that can be undertaken lightly, because for staff this may represent a change to their relationship with the organisation, and to the internal dynamics of the organisation, which some will welcome and some will resent. Unless there is a critical mass of staff among whom co-ownership can be established, there is always the danger for headteachers that their promotion of a development such as research engagement might be perceived as abusing their position to indulge their personal hobbies and interests.

Motivations and congruent funding sources

Chapter 4 identified four motivations or rationales for encouraging practitioner research – solving problems, modelling values, developing staff and enabling practitioner-led reform – although of course in practice all of these occur together in complex patterns.

At the more granular level, individual staff members engaging with practitioner research may have a wide range of motives, such as interest in a topic, or career progression aspirations.

School leaders have to take a position in relation to a wide range of individual cases. For example, they might produce a staff development policy which makes reference to the level of institutional support for particular kinds of practitioner research projects, and hence have to make judgements about what can be funded. These judgements could take account of the range of motivations for practitioner research and the range of possible funding models, and which matches are considered appropriate. Figure 6.1 offers a tool for making those decisions.

Funding
1. researcher's private time, no money needed
2. self-funded by researcher
3. research activity integrated into normal school or departmental budget
4. funded by partner higher education institution
5. grant-aided without 'strings'
6. sponsored with 'strings'
7. commissioned by third party: research under contract

Motivations
A. personal curiosity
B. individual professional and career development
C. team development of practice
D. school improvement (e.g. 'official' projects in school improvement plan)
E. evaluation of school practices and initiatives
F. production of 'transferable' techniques
G. to inform (or justify) policy (at school level or wider)
H. to inform the building of theory
I. to contribute to large or longitudinal data sets
J. to address issues identified by a sponsor or commissioner

	1	2	3	4	5	6	7
A							
B							
C							
D							
E							
F							
G							
H							
I							
J							

Which cells in the table represent appropriate combinations of motivation and funding source? Tick any that apply.

Figure 6.1 Motivations and congruent funding sources

Using this tool may help school leadership teams to avoid the extremes of policies that are either too accommodating (in using school resources to support research projects which are primarily advancing individuals' interests and career development) or too limiting (too sharply focused on institutional needs in a way that turns practitioner research into an almost managerial, mechanistic device for school improvement).

Chapter 8 suggests that the 'right' judgement on this matter ought, among other considerations, to take account of where the school is on its journey of development. The answer will differ between a school dealing with serious failure and a school riding on an established reputation for excellence.

Generally, the spirit of the practitioner research movement has been linked to empowerment. For that reason, a case may be made for suggesting that a school purporting to support practitioner research ought not to be discouraging to staff who want to pursue their own research interests; it may, however, be entirely reasonable not to fund that activity. The table in Figure 6.1 can also help school leadership teams to clarify the relationships they ought to be aiming for in respect of the school's involvement in externally initiated research activity.

Leaders' roles in including support staff in research engagement

In many schools, almost half (sometimes more than half) of the adults employed are people other than teachers, although that proportion, having risen dramatically over the last ten years, may well fall back as school budgets come under pressure. That being the case, it is interesting to examine the extent to which schools' claims to be 'communities of learning' (or similar descriptions) embrace their support staff. In some schools, doing so is a point of principle; in others, the headteacher, with embarrassed fidgeting, will start listing obstacles relating to conditions of service. If support staff are to be included in mutually beneficial ways in research engagement initiatives, the leadership and continuing active involvement of the headteacher is likely to be a necessary condition.

Some years ago an initiative by the College of Teachers supported classroom assistants in developing the skills of reflective practice. The College had made a successful application to the Esmée Fairbairn Foundation for funding to undertake the project. The College did not wish to duplicate existing courses for support staff; instead its purpose was to support the more general and longer-term nurturing of the skills and confidence of school support staff through reflective practice and peer group dialogue. To that end, the College supported the establishment of school-based practice development groups for teaching assistants, and at the same time investigated how such groups could best be sustained by school senior managers (Wilkins, 2005).

The support included development opportunities spread over three terms, including e-learning, supported self-learning through reflective practice, group discussions, school-based project work and portfolio-building with opportunities to achieve accreditation, and some limited face-to-face sessions with members of the College's professional development team. The research strand of the project drew upon baseline data, interviews with headteachers and participants, participation and completion rates, and the examination of portfolios produced by teaching assistants working in different school contexts. The research aimed to identify lessons both for school leaders and for the provision of external support for this kind of activity.

The project started with exploratory work spanning ten schools, of which six went on to form and sustain viable practice development groups of support staff. These six were all primary schools, ranging in size from 130 to 600 pupils. Four were in the East Midlands, one in South Yorkshire and one in South London. Some 73 participants in total achieved accreditations from the College; of these, 17 achieved ACoT (Associate of the College of Teachers) – a significant professional development award.

Among the six schools which engaged successfully with the project, a pattern became evident. From the comments of interviewees and from the proportion of participants achieving ACoT awards, the schools fell into two groups of three, distinguished by outcomes and positive perceptions. In three schools, the project could be described as moderately successful; in the other three it was definitely very successful. Each group of three embraced schools of different sizes and circumstances. The distinguishing factor was that in the latter group, the headteacher took personal involvement in supporting the project, typically by leading group sessions, advising the teaching assistants on their work, and taking a direct personal interest in its progress. The opportunity to work with the headteacher was clearly appreciated by some of the interviewees in these schools. The following comment by a participant is representative:

> The project has increased the self-esteem of the teaching assistants, by giving better understanding of their chosen study and more confidence in implementing it into current practice. The project has impacted on classroom practice…The headteacher made inputs to the project on behaviour, national curriculum and methods of research. It was good for him to have that time with us, to get all the TAs together. It made us stand back and look at what we were doing, and it was good to know that we could produce something that reached a standard and was worthwhile. It gave us the confidence to be learners.

The headteachers' direct involvement in these three schools was bound to be particularly helpful in enabling participants to develop the level of their reflective practice, project work and portfolio-building to the standards required for the ACoT award. The core of the project concerned the establishment and support of practice development groups *by the school*. The College's role as initiator, early facilitator and accrediting body had to strike the correct balance, keeping short of being seen as the external provider of a school-based course. In the three most successful schools, through the keen involvement of their headteachers, that balance was achieved.

In the other three schools, while the headteachers were supportive of the project, they were not directly involved. The work of leading and supporting the practice development group fell almost entirely on a senior teaching assistant designated for the purpose. Perceptions of benefit were still positive, but this approach limited the quality of the experience and the level of outcomes that could reasonably be achieved (Wilkins, 2005).

Research engagement for the motivation and effective deployment of long-serving staff

In the period 2001–04, two research projects took place regarding the motivation and effective deployment of older, long-serving teachers:

- The first was a pilot study funded by SAGA, a company specialising in a range of services for the 50+ age group, published as Wilkins and Head (2002).
- The second, building on this, was a national study commissioned and funded by the General Teaching Council for England (GTCE), with the support of SAGA, which was published as Wilkins *et al.* (2004). In this national study, examples of good practice were identified through a bottom-up process, which started with the stories of older teachers who believed that their school was making the best use of their experience.

The point that is relevant to this book is how often those teachers referred to being part of a school culture of reflection and improvement. Some of the case study schools had a large proportion of older and long-serving staff; they used a range of strategies for their development and effective deployment, such as involvement in initial teacher education, encouragement for external roles such as examining, job rotations, mentoring and team project work. At one school in particular, a large secondary school in rural Devon, the headteacher had given serious thought to the position of teachers aged 50+, working in partnership with the local authority (Devon County Council) and the University of Exeter. This was partly because nearly half of the staff were aged 50+, with more in their late forties. The strategies adopted had included job rotations, and involvement of the school in initial teacher education. The headteacher had gone on to establish 'The 50 Plus Club':

> We had a meeting with as many of the 50+s as could attend and said that there were a few projects we could work at...and we wanted ideas...One of them was to have a time of class contact remission, half a day a week, to pursue some interesting education-based projects with the University of Exeter.

> (Headteacher)

From this beginning grew a joint project between the school, the local authority, the university and the (then) Teacher Training Agency (which provided funding of around £15,000). This enabled the older teachers to conduct a range of action research projects addressing the school's educational priorities (Wilkins *et al.*, 2004).

Case study: Sweyne Park School

The ideas and experiences shared in this book span a period of ten years or so. It was important to add a contemporary example of a school exploring research engagement in the context of the issues current in the summer of 2010. Appendix 2 therefore presents a case study of Sweyne Park School in Rayleigh, Essex.

Sweyne Park was identified for this purpose by the author's colleague Sveta Mayer (introduced more fully in Chapter 7), who leads a school-based enquiry programme which forms two modules of a Master's degree. Dr Mayer had sensed that Sweyne Park was unusual in the extent to which this programme was nested within an established philosophy. The approach taken by the school's leadership was the strongest factor in supporting the school's research-engaged culture.

Conclusion

This chapter has shown that school leadership for research engagement is not a matter of adopting a particular leadership approach or style. It is likely to develop over a period of time as one manifestation of a leader's broader educational philosophy, and is likely to be in an interdependent relationship with a favourable organisational context.

One dimension of school leadership for research engagement is managing the interface with external sources of advice, support and accreditation for research engagement. This is explored in Chapter 7.

Chapter 7

External support for school research engagement

One of the recurrent themes of previous chapters is that research engagement by schools, if of sufficient quantity and quality to merit that description, is likely to be drawing upon one or more forms of external support. This chapter presents a case for increasing the capacity of research-engaged schools to become consciously discerning and proactive customers and commissioners of the external support upon which they draw. Without that, there will remain uncertainties about whose interests and agendas are having the most influence on particular developments.

In the definition of the research-engaged school offered in Chapter 1, one of the attributes included was that the characteristics of research engagement are sustained through the impetus of the school itself, rather than because the school is being 'done to' by external agencies. That expression conjures up intensive interventions to address school failure, or heavily prescriptive top-down initiatives. In addition there may be more subtle influences at work, which (albeit that they generally stem from good intentions) should nevertheless be raised so that schools can take a considered view in selecting their standpoint and response. This does, however, pose something of a 'chicken and egg' conundrum regarding how a school reaches the point at which it can exercise this discernment.

The field of external support for school research engagement is broad and complex, but at the same time much of its horsepower has been provided by a relatively small world of pioneering individuals, whose influence has been exerted through multiple channels. In addition to a range of specialised agencies, the main sources of external support include local authorities and higher education institutions – bodies with generic functions, which devote a small proportion of their energies to supporting research engagement by schools. In the same category is the General Teaching Council for England (GTCE) which, through its research department, has advocated research engagement (see, for example, the booklet *Using Research in Your School and Your Teaching*, GTCE, 2006), and which offers also the more specific support of its Teacher Learning Academy (TLA) initiative. (At the time of writing, the new national government has expressed the intention to abolish the GTCE, and for that reason the future of the TLA (which has a separate brand identity) is uncertain.)

Other sources of external support include organisations with remits for specific aspects of research engagement, such as the EPPI-Centre at the IOE, and the National Teacher Research Panel. These are examples: the total range of sources of relevant external support of one kind or another is vast.

The most effective support sometimes involves the combined impact of more than one source, most typically when local authorities have worked in partnership not just with schools but also with a university. Many of the forms of support described are either locality-specific, or thinly distributed, or depend upon the school either being referred to – or stumbling across – a website. According to its local context, the leadership team of an average school (i.e. a school chosen at random) interested in exploring the research-engaged route may well have no relevant and expert external support readily available to it at that early point beyond documentary guidance and resources obtained from websites. Usually, human agency plays its part in starting schools off on this journey. Individuals can make their own way: for example, taking a Master's programme with a research component opens up awareness and networks. The point is that a national picture of a vibrant 'industry' promoting and supporting research engagement by schools does not necessarily translate into an equivalent richness of opportunities at the local level.

It would be possible to attempt to provide a straightforward overview of the sources of external support, as indeed others have done from time to time, including the helpful summary produced by Hilary Street for the National Association of Head Teachers (Street, 2005), but any such overview would quickly become dated. One of the themes of this book's argument is that the research-engaged school should, as far as possible, be in the driving seat of its engagement with research. It seems right, therefore, to look at these sources of support in a way that places research-engaged schools as the central focus.

While there is no reason to doubt that all of the external sources of support have a primary motivation to benefit schools by meeting their needs in this area, it cannot be denied that way down in their priorities there are bound to be some secondary considerations: universities need to enrol students, award degrees, generate income, conduct research and produce publications; local authorities need to support school improvement and lead school systems; specialised organisations need to be seen to be engaging with a good number of users of their services. For their part, schools do not have research engagement as their top priority, because that will always be their pupils' learning and development. Nor will being a good customer to any particular supplier of external support feature high in their priorities, if at all, however warmly the word 'partnership' is applied to those transactions.

So in navigating this fast-developing marketplace of sources of external support for research-engaged schools, while it may be helpful to know what this or that university has been doing – or how the most active and progressive local authorities have been taking forward their work with schools; or what schemes and services can be subscribed to with other organisations; and what information is freely available – it is just as important to consider what schools want and need. Better information about what is available makes for more discerning consumer choices, but an additional change would be a shift from a sellers' to a buyers' market.

Schools' need for external support

But what do schools need? There are empirical studies which include information about the factors that help and hinder teachers engaged in and with research, and the sources of support that they find helpful. A major survey of this evidence as reported through published studies is Bell *et al.* (2010).

Thinking more specifically about a much smaller population than 'teachers engaged in and with research', namely schools where the leadership is actively pursuing developments to achieve the characteristics of a research-engaged school, the exploration of needs for external support can also be approached from first principles, by looking at the factors that have to be in place to engage successfully in a protracted process of significant change. These factors are generic, but in this context they apply mainly to senior and middle leaders in schools who want to increase the extent to which their school is research-engaged. This choice of approach also assumes that for the majority of schools, progressing to higher levels of research engagement does indeed represent a significant and protracted change. In short, people engaged in change need seven 'senses'. These are a 'sense':

- of desirable destination
- of motivation to progress towards that destination
- of navigable steps and milestones
- of ability and confidence to do what is required
- of permission to work differently
- of support from the organisation and the wider system
- that success will be marked by recognition in desirable ways.

The seven 'senses' offered above are distilled from the author's practical experience of consultancy, rather than from any specific empirical source or from scholarship, but inevitably these have resonances with ideas from literature, and it is worth drawing attention to two from the many which might come to readers' minds.

The first is Villa and Thousand's matrix for managing complex change in schools, developed from earlier work by Ambrose (1987), and offered in slightly different forms in several publications, including Villa and Thousand (1995) and Knoster *et al.* (2000). The matrix identified five factors essential to change:

- vision
- skills
- incentives
- resources
- action planning.

It also identified the consequences of each factor being absent (without vision, there is confusion; without skills, anxiety; without incentives, resistance; without resources, frustration; and without action planning, false starts or 'treadmill'). Of course in reality, it is not so much a matter of a single factor being wholly present or absent, but rather the extent and nature of weaknesses in each of the five factors and the consequential pattern of the problems to be addressed. Shortland-Jones *et al.* (2001) added a sixth factor, which seemed to them essential from the basis of their practical experience of change in schools: collegiality, the absence of which resulted in isolation.

There are clear connections to be charted between these factors and the seven 'senses' above. Vision feeds the sense of desirable destination; skills and resources relate to the senses of ability and confidence to do what is required, and permission to work differently; incentives are relevant (but see below) to motivation to progress towards the destination, and recognition of success; action planning supports navigable steps and milestones; and collegiality is part of the support from the organisation and the wider system.

A second connection is to the literature of motivation, for example McLean (2003), which, while being concerned primarily with how schools motivate their students, is intended to be applicable to school staff as well:

> *The principles outlined in this book will also be of relevance to school managers in their attempts to lead teaching staff and create a motivating school…management at all levels need to treat teachers the same way they expect teachers to treat their students.*
>
> (McLean, 2003: 5)

McLean drew attention to shifts in theories of motivation away from purely behavioural, with its emphasis on environmental factors (of which 'incentives' are one), towards greater recognition of the source of motivation being inside the person, including for example their goals and competency beliefs. So 'motivation is generated from inside while being heavily influenced from outside' (McLean, 2003), and beliefs, feelings and values influence behaviour.

McLean noted that the 'social climate of the [organisation] is a powerful motivator of academic as well as social behaviour', and that in each situation, a continuum of intrinsic and extrinsic motivations would be present (McLean, 2003: 9). Looking back at the seven 'senses' above, each will be subject to those continua, but extrinsic motivation is likely to be prominent in relation to navigable steps and milestones, permission to work differently, organisational support and recognition of success. Intrinsic motivation may play a greater part in relation to desirable destination, motivation to reach that destination and a sense of ability and confidence to do what is required.

External support for the seven 'senses'

For people who are not at the most senior levels of school leadership, the forms of support which generate these 'senses' come partly from within the organisation. One of the effects of external support ought to be to help school senior leadership teams to create these conditions, while also generating these 'senses' for the senior leaders. It is important to note, however, that most forms of external support for school research engagement impact on the practitioners who are engaged, regardless of their organisational level. For example, the most active interaction with external sources of support might be made by a group of relatively junior staff, or by the senior team, or by a cross-section, and these variations will tend to reflect the pattern of activity in the school, rather than differences in the forms of external support available.

In the comments below, the first six of the seven 'senses' have been grouped into pairs, because the patterns of external support currently available tend not to be calibrated finely enough to enable a worthwhile distinction to be drawn between the impacts of the support on each need within the pairs. In the following sections, needs for external support of varying kinds are identified; the main forms of support are then mapped against those needs; and issues affecting schools' levels of proactivity in relation to that support are identified.

Desirable destination; motivation

Anyone setting out on a journey of major change needs a clear vision, either of the intended destination, or at least of the intended direction of travel. This distinction is made because the more ambitious and visionary the aim, the more problematical it becomes to be very specific about the ultimate destination. The process of defining the ultimate destination can turn the vision either into something pedestrian or into something that can appear too idealistic to be capable of achievement. Also, if the journey involves going into unknown territory, any definition of ultimate destination must be provisional. That notwithstanding, a professional team contemplating a journey, such as one towards higher levels of research engagement, needs to know not only where they are going, but what it is that will be attractive about the destination. What benefits will accrue? In what ways, and to what extent, is that place really a better place than where they are now?

The second and separate need is for a sufficiently strong sense of motivation to commit to undertaking the journey. This involves both pull and push factors. The advantages of the desired destination need to be more than just beneficial in a general way: they need to generate in the individual a strong desire to participate in those benefits personally. On the 'push' side of the equation, motivation to move to somewhere different requires a sense of dissatisfaction with current location. For example, that dissatisfaction might be a growing awareness of, and frustration with, the paucity or poor quality of evidence about many aspects of school life to which the school leadership team claims to attach importance. These pull and push factors need to be linked, so that the individual identifies how moving to the desired destination will deal with the unsatisfactory elements of their current situation.

In the journey towards higher levels of research engagement by schools, the details of the ultimate destination are still somewhat hazy, because it is an evolving field of practice and those in the vanguard would be the first to say that there is scope to travel very much further.

The comments above assume that the desired destination of higher levels of research engagement, and motivation to move towards that destination, represent a conscious and collective decision: the headteacher and senior leaders seeing a distant land of promise and resolving to lead the school on a journey towards it. There is little evidence of how often this reflects real experiences in schools. Sometimes the process of research engagement builds up through the cumulative effect of individual choices and actions, and even those individuals may not at the time know quite where their journey will take them. A school may reach a point of momentum and critical mass when it finds itself 'research-engaged'. Chapter 1 spoke of the disjointed nature of intellectual journeys, and the journey towards school research engagement may sometimes be similar, but the school will still benefit from the same forms of external support.

What benefits from external support would help a school to meet the needs identified in this section? A school not yet in the vanguard but interested in moving forward and wanting to put some detail on its vision would find it useful to access descriptions of practices at schools further along the journey. To meet motivational needs, those descriptions must contain very robust evidence of the benefits of those practices, and those benefits need to be seen as relevant to the school's own circumstances.

School self-evaluation has a part to play in identifying benefits that might flow from a higher level of research engagement. Graham Handscomb has explored how reflective practice can contribute to the quality and effectiveness of school self-evaluation (Handscomb, 2008). The process of self-evaluation might include a focus on the range and quality of the evidence that the school is able to draw upon in arriving at its judgements: both internal evidence and evidence of practice at other schools, and how research engagement might be used to increase the extent and utility of that evidence. The process of school self-evaluation may also identify areas for school improvement where research engagement would be one of a suite of effective measures for bringing about the improvement.

What sources and forms of external support would provide those benefits? Accessible and trustworthy accounts of developments at schools further along the journey of research engagement would clearly be helpful, as might inspirational presentations by champions of research engagement, who can draw upon knowledge of leading-edge developments. Technical support with school self-evaluation would be helpful, if it could be provided from the specific standpoint of looking at improving the quality of evidence. Critical friendship, again if provided by someone with the necessary interests and skills, could hold up a mirror to the school so as, in the nicest possible way, to stimulate dissatisfactions to which research engagement would provide the remedies.

A source of support for schools, not only in relation to their visioning, but also in relation to other needs discussed in the following sections, has been the National Teacher Research Panel (NTRP, 2011). The NTRP has offered a range of informative papers and opportunities for interaction, including through conferences and publications in which school-based researchers are able to share their experience. Through its constitution, the NTRP has been, at least in formal terms, owned by the 'movement' of school-based research. It has, however, been sponsored by government, the General Teaching Council for England, the National College for the Leadership of School and Children's Services, and the Learning and Skills Improvement Service, so perhaps the NTRP is best understood as a meeting point of top-down and bottom-up perspectives. At the time of writing, its future has been rendered uncertain by the policies of the new UK Government.

As previously noted, the field of school research engagement is led by influential individuals. One of these is Philippa Cordingley (see, for example, Cordingley (2004) for her perspective on some of the issues covered in this book). Philippa Cordingley is a former senior education officer and consultant, who established CUREE, the Centre for the Use of Research and Evidence in Education, which is a specialised consultancy. She has been a significant influence on the development of the NTRP: she was its founding champion, she is its professional adviser and facilitator, and CUREE is its source of administrative support.

An issue for school leadership teams at this stage of the research engagement journey is how to make meaningful judgements about the information and advice that may be encountered. The more professional reading they are able to undertake, the more time they are able to devote to peer discussion of that reading, and the more they are able to take account of a range of viewpoints, then the better placed they will be to engage critically and constructively with new knowledge and suggestions. The services of the NTRP emphasise interaction and are supportive of those aims.

Navigable stages; ability

As with any other significant change, the development of a higher level of research engagement represents a daunting prospect for practitioners who have not been used to working in that way. Research engagement involves not only new activity, but also the development and application of new skills. That new way of working has either to be substituted for the old way, or time has to be found so that research engagement can be 'done' as an extra activity on top of the 'day job'.

While many would say that the first option is theoretically correct and in keeping with the notion of evidence-based professional practice, opinions are divided as to how realistic it is to expect busy practitioners to produce research of any real worth without investing significant extra time: an issue reconsidered later in this chapter. Some practitioners may perceive this new and different way of working as too hard a step to take. Others may take a deep breath and 'plunge in', and then become frustrated with what they are able to achieve. Of course, as with other new practices, serious research engagement has to be worked towards through logical steps and stages, involving the cumulative development of skills and understanding, opportunities to practise before moving towards more complex applications, and points at which small, early successes can be celebrated.

School leaders who lead the process need to be able to present and explain these stages and milestones at the outset, in a way that conveys realistic expectations of the inputs and timescales that are likely to be required. This will not only lead to better understanding of what research engagement will 'look like' and its worth, but more importantly will enable people to make choices about which steps and stages are achievable for them personally. If the aim is to generate a large enough group of actively involved staff to be effective as a supportive peer group and as an agency for change, then it is likely that the 'steps and stages' will need to be differentiated to offer a range of options to suit different career stages, academic aspirations and levels of time commitment.

If this can be achieved, it will create the confidence that people need to feel when they are embarking on change. But unless that confidence is matched by a parallel process of skills development, it may turn out to be false confidence. People may busy themselves with activity to which they attach the vocabulary of research, and which they believe, quite mistakenly, has merit and significance. Or they may have a good appreciation of what is required, but give up in frustration, finding it too hard, because they have underestimated the need to develop their skills. So those leading the change require a thorough and authoritative understanding of the skills needs associated with each step of the journey, and the means to provide the development that will generate those skills effectively.

What benefits from external support would help a school to meet the needs identified in this section? Other than in the rare cases where the school staff includes leaders who are seasoned experts in research engagement, including supporting practitioner research projects, external sources of support are required for advice and guidance on:

- the nature of activities that might usefully be undertaken
- the steps, stages and timescales involved
- the skills needed at each stage
- the developmental activities which will produce those skills.

External support is also needed for ongoing expert technical support and quality assurance of the research engagement activity, especially for practitioner research projects. These functions include guidance on the ethical aspects of school-based research. Another benefit from external support is access to the stories and experience of other practitioners who are further along the journey.

What sources and forms of external support would provide those benefits? Usually, the most obvious source of the relevant technical expertise for general guidance and for skills development is university-based personnel. The form of the support may often be an accredited programme, which, if it is not entirely school-based, will also give participants the benefit of a wider peer group and network, enabling them to see and evaluate their own activities within a broader field. Another source of support which would normally be additional to (rather than alternative to) the first is the collaborative 'networks', 'learning communities' and so on operated by groups of schools either at their own initiative or with the support of the local authority. These may be particularly helpful in providing an extended peer group who are familiar with the local context.

University-based initiatives have included the Centre for Applied Research in Education at the University of East Anglia, which was established in 1970 as a development of the previous Humanities Curriculum Project, and which still exists as a research and research training centre.

In 1976, CARN was established – the Collaborative Action Research Network – which continues to flourish, publishing the journal *Educational Action Research* and providing visibility, support and networking for systematic, critical and creative inquiry. Its work was recently reviewed by Bridget Somekh, one of its main long-term champions (Somekh, 2010).

Another supportive network is the Canterbury Action Research Network (CANTARNET) operated by Canterbury Christ Church University. As its website explains, CANTARNET was established in 1996 as a support network for those taking Canterbury Christ Church University's school-based MA in School Development:

> Teachers and other education professionals are supported in initiating and managing change in their own schools, based upon systematic inquiry integrated with their everyday practice. The focus of the work is derived from individuals' own concerns and responsibilities, negotiated within the context of school development priorities. Academic study through connection with the University enables teachers to support their work with wider research, and test theory in practice in order to develop new knowledge and understanding in their own professional contexts.
>
> (www.canterbury.ac.uk)

This brief neatly encapsulates the 'manifesto' of the teacher-led development movement and provides an example of regional provision of events, publications and contacts which support school-based enquiry.

An issue for school leadership teams is that while support offered through networks of the kind illustrated above offers choice as to how, and how far, to be involved, other kinds of external support can take forms that might be perceived as 'package deals', or almost as 'branded products'. Where the support takes the form of a university-accredited programme, it will come with set requirements; there are numerous different options; and sometimes several are available from the same institution. Inevitably, the individual who is the point of contact tends to be most enthusiastic about the programme they work on or know best. Schools need to shop around and also to keep focused on the needs and interests which they identified, rather than being too readily distracted by the attractions of what they are being offered, which may actually focus on a somewhat different set of aims. Some compromise may be necessary, however, and often the school's own thinking will develop as a result of the dialogue.

If the point of this external support includes accessing knowledge and quality assurance, then it may be worth checking how the source of support positions itself in relation to the debates reviewed in Chapter 5. For example, will participants be expected to shoehorn their activity into the understandings of validity and reliability applied within conventional academic research? Or will they be encouraged and assisted in applying the 'new validity criteria' of Anderson and Herr (1999), which are more appropriate to school-based practitioner enquiry?

A separate issue is whether, to what extent and by what means the form of external support will build the capacity of the school leadership team in the field of research engagement. Overgenerous use of terms such as 'partnership' and 'collaboration' can cloud this issue. Schools need to check out whether the form of external support foregrounds specific processes for capacity-building, or whether the reality is that the school will be signing up to be 'done to' for the next few years in ways that maintain a dependency relationship.

Permission; support

Undertaking a process of significant and protracted change within an organisation also requires a sense of 'permission' to work in new and different ways and a sense of support. This support is not just in terms of receiving the practical help and co-operation required, but rather the sense of assurance on the part of the person doing things differently that at some future point, perhaps when problems arise, the organisation (or the wider system) will not turn on them and criticise them for their actions.

A school wanting to move to higher levels of research engagement can convey the sense of 'permission' to its staff by the strong, ongoing and visible patronage of this method of working by the senior leadership team, and by its inclusion in school development plans and in the objectives negotiated with individuals as part of their performance management.

The sense of support can be conveyed by:

- enabling a critical mass of staff to be actively participating in research engagement
- constructing the timetable so as to allow sufficient opportunities for relevant activity and discussions
- giving space and respect to research-related matters in official meetings
- ensuring that the governing body is aware of, and fully supportive of, what staff are doing in this area
- providing a staff reference library
- prioritising research-related continuing professional development and providing reasonable levels of financial support for this
- operating a risk-accepting, no-blame professional culture.

What benefits from external support would help a school to meet the needs identified in this section? While a school, from its own resources and through its own choices, can go a long way towards creating the senses of permission and support for research engagement among its own personnel, at institutional level, the school as an organisation can only meet these needs through external support. This factor is closely connected to the issue of recognition, which is dealt with in the next section.

What sources and forms of external support would provide those benefits? Under current conditions, the attitude of the local authority is important as a potential source of permission and support, especially in those local authorities which have taken a serious interest in school research engagement. Under the emerging policy environment this factor may become less relevant to an increasing proportion of schools, as government policies encourage them to distance themselves from local democracy. Making formalised linkages between research engagement at school level and national schemes (such as the Teacher Learning Academy), national agencies (such as the Training and Development Agency for Schools (TDA) or the Specialist Schools and Academies Trust) or individual universities can provide a sense of legitimacy and hence permission. External funding streams provide their own, very distinct, form of permission and support. Finally, for headteachers, a like-minded peer group can go some way to meeting these needs.

In addition to the range of agencies mentioned, sources of these kinds of support can include:

- collaborative networks, including some run by universities specifically to encourage practitioner research
- School Improvement Partners in the cases where they understand and support school research engagement
- charitable foundations that can be sources of funding.

An issue for school leadership teams is that while these sources of support may be helpful in other, more general ways, they do not amount to very much in relation to the specific senses of 'permission and support' as outlined above. Organisations and agencies which provide advice and 'frameworks' do not generally take on much responsibility towards the schools that use their products or buy into their logo. In this matter, as with so many others, school leadership teams are heavily accountable in the event of anything going wrong. The main thing likely to 'go wrong' in relation to school research engagement is if individuals, groups or the whole organisation allow their interest in research to distract their attention from their primary responsibility for the achievement and well-being of their students.

So the words 'permission' and 'support' are really shorthand for reassurance and confirmation that the research activities that people are undertaking are relevant and justifiable in the context of their current professional priorities. External project funding from a reputable body, while offering a powerful sense of 'permission', can be a mixed blessing. It reinforces the belief that research engagement is an extra that requires extra funding, which does not help those who argue the cause of evidence-informed professional practice. There is then always the issue of how much of the good work can be embedded and sustained after the funding finishes.

Recognition

Finally, people undertaking significant long-term change need a sense that success will be marked by recognition in desirable ways. This factor can be considered at the individual level and at the institutional level. Very often these are aligned, in that the research-engaged school will take a certain amount of credit for the recognitions achieved by individuals that the school has supported.

For individuals, the recognitions that act as motivators to research engagement include:

- the achievement of academic and professional qualifications
- career advancement
- opportunities to present work to internal and external meetings, including presenting papers at conferences
- opportunities to contribute to publications.

For many teachers, seeing the ideas generated through their research being put into practice with good outcomes for students, with some public acknowledgement, is the most rewarding form of recognition.

For the school as an institution, the rewards and recognitions for research engagement are inextricably tied up with the school's overall success, as measured by students' attainment, Ofsted inspection ratings, and the school's ability to attract and retain able staff. From the point of view of a school senior leadership team, those outcomes are their own reward; they are also a necessary condition if the school is to continue to enjoy a sense of 'permission' to be pursuing an interest in research engagement. A valued accolade is when external quality assurance agencies, such as Ofsted or Investors in People, appear to acknowledge a connection between activities of research engagement and the achievement of high ratings.

What benefits from external support would help a school to meet the needs identified in this section? The benefit of external recognition is that it validates the school's view that what it is doing is worthwhile: corroborating those opinions and judgements and converting what would otherwise be collective self-praise into 'facts' that become matters of public record.

What sources and forms of external support would provide those benefits?

Clearly, accreditations of individuals' work provide a tangible form of recognition. These may be primarily academic qualifications, as awarded by universities, or primarily professional qualifications, for example those awarded by the College of Teachers.

These are individual recognitions. At the whole-school level, building upon the National Research Engaged Schools Project, the National Foundation for Educational Research (NFER) has developed a research-engaged school/

college award scheme, which judges submissions against 22 assessment criteria.

In addition to accreditations, other forms of recognition include the acceptance of papers at conferences and articles in publications such as professional journals. Learned societies, professional associations, conference-organising bodies, universities and publishers are among the organisations that have the potential to be sources of external support with this. Schools often find the easiest way to present their work at significant conferences is as part of a symposium session organised by a university or an interest group. Another form of recognition is the involvement of school staff in externally organised professional development in the field of research engagement, as a speaker at INSET (in-service education and training) events, or as an associate tutor on a university programme. All of these examples provide external endorsement of quality.

An issue for school leadership teams is that most forms of external recognition for research engagement require the school to adopt an outward-facing orientation, which is why that should be one of the attributes in the definition of a research-engaged school.

Balancing recognition against school priorities

Another issue is the balances that need to be struck between achieving recognitions and doing what the school really wants to do. Chapter 5 commented on situations where the 'tail' of accreditation can wag the 'dog' of enquiry-based professional practice: often there is much to be said for getting the latter established first. Usually, external recognitions involve adopting systems and methods that are often helpful but can also be binding. For example, at Sweyne Park School (see the case study in Appendix 2), which has been, and continues to be, committed to being a thinking school, for a long time one of the policy aims had been to achieve the Thinking School Award operated by the University of Exeter, but the decision was reached not to do so, because 'it would involve using a prescribed package'.

Another issue concerns the sensitive subject of organisational micro-politics, and a need to challenge the assumption that all forms of external endorsement are always helpful to the organisation, and that everything in the research-engaged garden is fragrant. Some people follow their own interests in ways that oppose or undermine their organisation's senior management. As noted in Chapter 1, uncertainty can arise regarding whether the interpretations of reality conveyed in accounts of practitioner research would be shared by other key stakeholders. More widely, when university assessors are awarding Master's degrees, there is usually no place in the process for checking out whether the project and its conclusions were seen as welcome and helpful by the candidate's headteacher. The same applies to the way that conference papers are accepted. So it is not particularly difficult for a maverick element in the organisation to use external endorsement of its research activities to wrong-foot the leadership and to gain support and momentum for their standpoint, knowing that the leadership would look bad if it expressed a negative view of these 'achievements'. It is easier to design out such hazards in organisations where the leadership team is actively driving both the organisation's professional culture and the agenda of research engagement.

Some accredited programmes take pains to ensure that the enquiry activity they accredit has involved the institution, rather than merely the individual. One way to do so is through the expectation that candidates for higher degrees will give convincing evidence that their work is well supported by 'the new validity criteria' (Anderson and Herr, 1999), as summarised in Chapter 5. The MA in School Development programme offered by Canterbury Christ Church University, for example, requires viable school-based groups and an active in-school co-ordinator, raising the likelihood that the work that participants submit for accreditation will carry a reasonable level of institutional support (in the form of 'dialogic validity' – Anderson and Herr).

Case study of collaborative enquiry

Another distinctive example of such a programme has been reported by Sveta Mayer (Mayer, 2009, 2010). This programme had its origins in the Networked Learning Communities (NLCs) programme of the National College for School Leadership, and the funded Postgraduate Professional Development (PPD) scheme of the TDA. Mayer was involved in brokering the development of a partnership project between The Learning Initiative and the IOE, to offer a school-based collaborative inquiry programme, the costs of which would be covered by the PPD funding stream. The programme was validated as a Master's level double module called 'Leading inquiry based professional learning communities'. (Before moving on, at this point it is necessary temporarily for the rest of this section to abandon consistent distinction between UK English and American English usages of 'enquiry' and 'inquiry' in order to quote sources that adopt the American usage.)

In contrast to the individual project by a lone practitioner researcher that some programmes require, this programme requires the participant to lead a process (as 'lead inquirer') involving others: 'inquiry advocates', who support and mentor the lead inquirer; 'practitioner inquirers', who conduct inquiry under guidance; and 'inquiry assistants', who participate in inquiry under guidance. This means that the participant must get others involved in a structured way, and that those who might normally be designated as the subjects of research are co-opted as 'inquiry assistants'. As it is a school-based programme, there has to be a viable group in a school for it to operate, which means that each participant has to designate these roles in relation to their inquiry.

Mayer (2010) reported that these arrangements worked best where the participant was prepared to:

- delegate and share decisions
- involve relevant others as co-designers and co-researchers
- share vision and strategy by listening to and incorporating others' views
- be flexible in the interests of collaboration
- ensure mutual benefit as well as benefit to school development.

Mayer's study found that the model offered by this programme was significantly helpful to the building of inquiry-based communities in schools; that such inquiry increased the evidence used to inform practice; that it gave teachers a sense of empowerment; and that the focus on teacher development and school improvement was helpful to the collaboration between the schools and the higher education institution (Mayer, 2010).

Books and articles quite properly describe support for school research engagement as coming from, for example, a university, a local authority, the GTCE or another body, but of course in reality that support comes from individuals, some of whom have made major contributions to their organisation's work in this field, such as Lesley Saunders at the GTCE, or Graham Handscomb at Essex County Council, or Philippa Cordingley though CUREE and the NTRP. Many of the individuals supporting research engagement developed parts of their thinking during a career phase as a school-based practitioner. Looking at individuals can help to offset some of the connotations that go with institutional labels. Sveta Mayer's own story is interesting. The following information was provided in an interview conducted in summer 2010.

Sveta Mayer trained as a scientist, taking a degree in biological sciences and a PhD in chemotherapy at King's College London. Then she combined a lectureship in pharmacology with post-doctoral research in neuro-pharmacology at King's College London and the University of Kentucky, USA, looking into the molecular effects of drugs used for alleviating withdrawal effects from alcoholism, which meant studying the part of the brain concerned with learning and memory. At the end of the research scholarship, her growing interest in the brain gave her an appetite to learn more, so she decided to take a year out to gain an MSc in neuroscience at the Institute of Psychiatry, London, whereupon she considered her career options:

Lecturing made me realise I loved teaching. How could I combine being a research neuroscientist and an aspiring teacher? I wanted to continue researching into learning and memory. How? Back in the laboratory? That takes decades from in vitro to application. I wanted more direct involvement. I decided my laboratory ought to be the classroom. I needed to embed myself and do insider research in a school. So I decided to do teacher training and seek employment in a school.

These explorations led to Sveta joining the Graduate Teacher Programme at a school which was supportive of her aims and which had funding for research through the NCSL's Networked Learning Communities (NLCs) scheme. Within a year, Sveta became an NCSL Research Advocate and began overseeing the research work of the six schools in the NLC, as well as pursuing her own research. The research funding through the NLC project lasted for four years. At the end of that period, Sveta was part of a group that obtained funding through the TDA's PPD scheme. This group became Networked Learning Partnerships, which later turned into The Learning Institute. Sveta had been school-based for six years and decided to move from that to a consultancy role with Networked Learning Partnerships, thence to the negotiation of the double module described earlier, and in due course into an academic appointment at the IOE.

One of the factors in Sveta's decision not to stay in her school concerned changes at that institution:

One option was to develop the school I was in as a research hub as a base from which to run the PPD programme. But the school was restructuring and re-prioritising and this didn't include this aim. The school wasn't ready to be a research hub; I would have had to push very hard to make it happen, with no guarantee of success.

This illustrates how school contexts can change in ways that become less favourable for research engagement. Long-term stability and continuity of commitment is an important factor, as Sveta affirmed in relation to the programme she currently leads, described above:

Where there is a stable culture, this programme has been highly successful. Where it is not stable, the participants have continued their masters module but the collaborative communities begin to collapse during the module itself. Also, as well as culture, where there is stability of the senior leadership team and headship it has worked well; where there have been changes, the programme wasn't successful.

It was clear that, although she had put a lot of thought and application into her own research, the biggest area of Sveta's professional satisfaction had come from supporting other research-engaged teachers and making the network a success. That success was summarised in a conference paper written by Sveta and her colleagues, outlining and showing the links between the projects in each school, which was presented to the NCSL's NLCs Conference. Regarding the outcomes of her own research over that six-year period, she said:

> *I took it to various points of understanding. I couldn't give research*
> *the time I had envisaged.*

As noted earlier, there are different opinions about whether it is practicable for teachers to undertake research of worthwhile scope and standard without investing considerable extra time into working in that way either through remission from normal duties or through the use of discretionary time. For example, the following was McIntyre's considered conclusion:

> *But teachers can reasonably be asked to engage seriously in research*
> *only if their conditions of work change radically: their schools need to*
> *be firmly led and committed to being, in a serious sense, researching*
> *schools; teachers themselves can do serious research only if they are*
> *asked to do much less of other things, such as classroom teaching;*
> *they must be given time and other resources for research; they must*
> *be supported in learning to do research and in doing it; the social*
> *organisation of schools must facilitate collaborative research; and it*
> *must be rewarding for teachers to do research.*
>
> (McIntyre, 2008: 40–1)

Attractive as it may be to press the case for 'working differently' as the preferable approach, increasing pressures on teachers mean that it is now appropriate to hear the voice of realism speaking more distinctly. If a teacher with the academic credentials and motivation of Sveta Mayer had problems finding the necessary time, then that suggests the problem is real.

External support from local authorities

One of the publications to come out of the National Research Engaged Schools Project 'Investigating the research-engaged school' (Sharp *et al.*, 2005) was a booklet summarising the project's findings regarding the role of local authorities (Sharp *et al.*, 2006b).

Having adopted the aim of making the research-engaged school the central focus of this chapter's review of external support for research-engaged schools, it is noteworthy that the first section of this booklet (Sharp *et al.*, 2006b) itemises the advantages *to the local authority* of schools being research-engaged. The latter parts of the booklet extend this theme, recording how the project caused some local authority personnel to become enthusiastic about making their own work more research-engaged, concluding with a section entitled 'Towards a research engaged local authority?'.

Research engagement is desirable at every level of the education system, including local authorities, but from the viewpoint of a school seeking external support for its research engagement, it is important for there to be a mutual clarity of understanding about who is in the driving seat, whose agendas are being pursued, and who is serving whom. The booklet lists the ways in which local authorities can support whole-school research engagement, which its authors group under the headings: 'Initiating research engagement'; 'Connecting school research teams'; and 'Embedding research engagement'. That list has been regrouped below under the headings used earlier in this chapter.

Desirable destination; motivation

- Explaining the concept
- Encouraging schools to take part
- Providing leadership and challenge
- Using research to take forward new initiatives

Navigable stages; ability

- Connecting schools with similar research themes
- Ensuring schools have access to information and research evidence
- Growing research engagement in schools through communities of practice
- Building capacity: people with research and mentoring skills
- Ensuring research is included in continuing professional development

Permission; support

- Providing support
- Valuing enquiry and research
- Ensuring research is used and valued in the local authority

Recognition

- Encouraging teams to share their work at school, area and national levels

These forms of support can be seen to be well distributed in relation to schools' needs. Sharp *et al.* (2006b) also included, under their heading 'Connecting school research teams', the functions of networking between local authority staff and schools, and connecting the local authority, schools and higher education institutions, which seem to be methods through which the benefits as listed are brought about.

The forms of support identified by Sharp *et al.*, and illustrated in the booklet by examples, were all taken from the National Research Engaged Schools Project, which involved five local authorities: Birmingham, Essex, Hertfordshire, Oldham and West Sussex. These were involved in the project because of their interest and leading-edge practices in this field. While it is good to celebrate this work, and to show what some local authorities are doing, findings like these leave a major open question in their implications: to what extent could, and should, local authorities generally adopt similar methods of working? This is an important question for schools in the other 170 local authorities with education powers in England and Wales, for whom it might translate as: 'If we decide to become a more research-engaged school, is it reasonable for us to expect our local authority to develop the kinds of support that were reported in this study?'

The Preface mentioned that prior to the National Research Engaged Schools Project, the Local Government Association had commissioned a previous relevant study from NFER. This was *Using Research for School Improvement: The LEA's role* (Wilson *et al.*, 2003). A survey of all 175 English and Welsh education authorities had identified eight which had strategies in place to encourage the use of research. The research consisted of case studies of each of these local authorities. They were: Birmingham, Bristol, Hammersmith and Fulham, Lancashire, Merthyr Tydfil, Oldham, Rochdale and West Sussex. Three of these also took part subsequently in the National Research Engaged Schools Project. The arrangements for research utilisation in five of these authorities (Birmingham, Bristol, Lancashire, Merthyr Tydfil and West Sussex) involved a university partner.

Involvement in action research was identified as an important means of engaging teachers with research. This needed to be resourced, relevant and practical, collaborative, teacher-owned, and accredited or otherwise recognised (Wilson *et al.*, 2003). The report made recommendations to local authorities wishing to facilitate the use of research for school improvement. These included: establishing a clear lead role; resourcing; promoting collaboration and wider partnerships; embedding research engagement within school improvement initiatives; and establishing an evidence-informed culture that encourages teachers to question existing practice (Wilson *et al.*, 2003).

Reconsidering both of these reports (Sharp *et al.*, 2006b; Wilson *et al.*, 2003) in 2010 identifies two major limitations:

- One is simply the reduced scope and capacity of local government. Over the last five years or so, local authority advisory services have been greatly reduced and have had to focus more sharply on specific central government priorities. More recently, the combination of the ending of central government's National Strategies, cuts in public spending, and the new Government's commitment to removing as many schools as possible from local democracy have sent that trend almost into freefall.

- The second limitation concerns the implicit assumption (not on the part of the authors of either of these research reports) that there can be 'lateral transfer of good practice' (as advocated, for example, in many of the writings of David Hargreaves) in a matter such as this, along the lines of 'these five (or eight) authorities have worked in this way, therefore any number of the other 170 (or 167) could do so'. As with practitioner research undertaken by teachers, where the 'practice' cannot be separated from the practitioner, so it is with the research engagement strategies developed by certain local authorities. These were the work of specific individuals who were interested in and motivated to develop these ways of working, often over a period of many years, and in a context that was favourable but is bound to become increasingly difficult.

Putting these two factors together, there seems little alternative but to conclude that in those local authorities which passed through the last two decades without being noticeably enthused about stimulating and supporting school research engagement, the chance that they will, in the foreseeable future, develop the interest to do so (combined with the means to do so effectively) is virtually zero. So, for schools located away from the relatively small proportion of local authorities that currently have strong practice in this field, it is unrealistic to expect very much support from their local authority for their journey towards higher levels of research engagement.

External support through networks

Another source of (mainly mutual) support is through networks of schools that have research as one of their aims.

McLaughlin *et al.* (2008) have researched what is currently known (which they conclude to be 'very little indeed' (p.81)) about the relationship between school networks and school research engagement, especially the ways in which networks can support action research projects undertaken by teachers. McLaughlin *et al.* trace: the growth in the popularity of school networks as a device promoted by government and its agencies; the problems of definition; and some of the tensions and problems in school networks. They critique the 'taken for granted' good of school networks:

> There is, it seems, little reporting of 'bad' or 'weak' school networks, or evidence regarding whether networking is necessarily the 'best' means by which to accomplish a particular set of ends. This sometimes unquestioning belief in the intrinsic rightness of school networks may

detract from a more useful and rigorous critique of what does and does not work well, and why.
(Black-Hawkins, 2008a: 65)

McLaughlin *et al.* presented (among other, wider research material) case studies of six of the networked learning communities (NLCs) in the UK, which formed part of the NCSL's NLC initiative. These were chosen from the larger population of NLCs:

because they were considered to be actively engaged in practitioner research and enquiry. Therefore, the case studies were expected to explore what was working well rather than examine how and why some networks were less successful in their research endeavours.
(Black-Hawkins, 2008b: 112)

In the first case study, 'the image of a team and a captain was used to describe the central role' of the local authority consultant, whose support was considered vital. The second case study network was built on an existing and well-established Education Action Zone (a government initiative giving funding to groups of schools in challenging areas). The Education Action Zone-funded infrastructure included full-time staff, and the active roles of the director and assistant director of the Zone in supporting research was considered crucial. The third case study had not drawn on structured external support to any significant extent, although 'the NLC national link person was highly valued...and often gave more of his time than was allotted'. This study reported a number of challenges that had been experienced, to which more external support might have been helpful. The fourth case study was of an NLC that was also an existing and well-established partnership between a group of schools and a university, which continued after the end of the funded NLC project. The fifth case study had also benefited from a link that had been developed with a higher education institution (HEI):

The research training provided by the HEI had been crucial to the success of research activities, offering useful technical skills and knowledge to teachers as well as developing their confidence. It had also allowed a shared language and understanding across the group of researchers, thus supporting their learning as a network.
(Black-Hawkins, 2008c: 155)

The sixth case study was of an NLC formed by a group of schools (spread across a wide area) that were all special schools, specialising in meeting the needs of students with severe learning difficulties. The network had intended to embrace the local authority and a university, but those links had not been developed. Research and enquiry were still at an early stage of development at the time of the study.

The NCSL's NLCs were a funded project with central support: this put them in a more favourable position than an unsupported network of schools simply deciding to work together. These six case studies where research 'was working well' are consistent with the view that research-engaged schools need external support whether or not they are part of a mutually supportive network of schools. There is nothing in McLaughlin *et al.* (2008) to suggest that networks of schools could provide a substitute for the kinds of support for research engagement that have been provided by local authorities, government and its agencies, and universities. There is little prospect that the contribution of local authorities will show an overall increase: it is far more likely to decline. The new national Government in the UK is committed to reducing the scale of activity and spending by government and its agencies. For example, the kinds of support for research engagement that have been provided from time to time by NCSL (now NCLSCS) and by the TDA are unlikely to be seen again for a long while – if at all.

The future path for the development of school research engagement is likely to depend quite heavily on the kinds of partnerships that will be formed between groups of schools and universities. What agendas – and whose agendas – will guide that path? This question is explored in Chapter 8.

Research engagement: Whose agenda?

Chapter 1 suggested that a coherent view of school research engagement might achieve clarity not just in relation to the questions 'what?' and 'how?', but also on 'why?', 'to what ends?' and 'to whose ends?'. The intervening six chapters have conveyed a perspective of the research-engaged schools 'movement', and have identified some of the complexities and conundrums that arise in relation to that activity. Issues of motives and purposes may be identified at all levels – from whole-school systems, to institutions, sections or departments within institutions, and right down to the individual level. This chapter takes the factors of motives and purposes to a further stage of consideration, and in so doing, offers some maps on which to locate the issues.

At the level of whole systems, reference has been made to national developments and debates, including initiatives by governments to increase the relevance of educational research and its impact on practice. That means, of course, 'relevance' to issues that the government of the day and its agencies have selected as important; 'impact on practice' means forms of impact that will endorse and implement – or at least be not repugnant to – prevailing political perspectives on school and classroom operational practices.

Also at the system level are differences in aims as between, for example, top-down and bottom-up interpretations of 'evidence-based practice', and their associated inclinations towards either 'engineering' or 'enlightenment' understandings of the relationship between research and practice. Comments in Chapter 7 about external sources of support for school research engagement acknowledged that, as well as their primary aim to support schools, some of these sources of support also, inevitably, have secondary motivations concerned with their own survival, profile and influence.

At the institutional level, a range of motives lead some people to become research-engaged, or to encourage research engagement.

Chapters 1 and 5 indicated that research engagement inevitably affected the micro-political manoeuvrings of individuals and groups within schools as organisations. Chapter 4 illustrated, through case studies, research engagement led in part by the motives of problem-solving, promoting professional development, 'living' and exemplifying an educational philosophy, and supporting teacher-led reform. Chapter 6 considered the role of school leaders as supporters of research engagement, and acknowledged the range of organisational management aims that can act as motivators in that process.

At the level of the individual deciding to become research-engaged, Chapter 6 suggested a wider range of motives, such as career development, or finding a topic intrinsically interesting.

Chapter 8 now takes the factors of motives and purposes a little further, by widening the focus to include two additional areas for consideration.

The first concerns the positioned nature of the research process itself. As will be expanded upon later, the notion of objectivity in research is, according to viewpoint, either problematical, or unattainable or undesirable. Many of the fields of educational research with which school-based practitioners may become engaged are themselves far from objective. These fields include lines of enquiry which have their positioned agendas and positioned genres. Individuals becoming engaged with research will generally, given free and informed choice, gravitate towards topics, lines of enquiry and literatures that resonate with their normative values, political beliefs and view of the world; with what they want to do with their lives.

The second focus is the more workaday connection between school research engagement as an activity, and perceived priorities for school development and improvement. Except for those who subscribe to very mechanistic and managerial views of the work of schools, those perceptions also will not be entirely objective, but will reflect the educational philosophies of school leaders. Understanding the relationship between school research engagement and school development involves recognising the positioned nature of research fields, and of approaches to school development, and of the individuals involved in these processes in their capacity as political human beings. Doing so points towards mapping school research engagement in relation to three other aspects of the landscape (to extend the topographical metaphor): the broad aims and purposes of education and the school system; strategies for school development and improvement; and the shaping of ideas through the literatures and lines of enquiry pursued within particular fields of study. School research engagement does not lend itself to comprehensive survey, so any 'map' will be like the products of early cartographers, with misshapen coastlines, 'terra incognita' and 'here be dragons'.

Empowerment, agency and individual responsibility

Karl Popper's seminal exploration of the 'open society' can be interpreted as promoting a sense of individual responsibility and 'agency' (i.e. a belief that actions will result in outcomes); an appreciation of personal standpoint in enquiry; and a sense of moral purpose for each generation to build responsibly on the legacy it inherits (Popper, 1966). His emphasis on 'agency' was a counter to the fatalistic stance of historicism:

> *The historicist substitutes for a rational question: 'What are we to choose as our most urgent problems, how did they arise, and along what roads may we proceed to solve them?' the irrational and apparently factual question: 'Which way are we going? What, in essence, is the part that history has destined us to play?'*
>
> (Popper, 1966, Vol. 2: 268)

> *Neither nature nor history can tell us what we ought to do. Facts...cannot determine the ends we are going to choose... Institutions...are not rational, but we can decide to fight to make them more rational...We can make it our fight for the open society and against its enemies...It is up to us to decide what shall be our purpose in life.*
>
> (Popper, 1966, Vol. 2: 278)

The acceptance of individual responsibility, sense of agency and moral purpose are closely linked. Fullan (1993) has emphasised moral purpose as a key driver of educational change. The growth of action research by teachers, and broader concepts of teacher-led development (Frost and Durrant, 2003), have been predicated on assumptions of responsibility and agency. Often, moral purpose will have a part in driving that activity, and in this context, moral purpose will be connected to beliefs about the purposes of education and schooling. Implicit in moral purpose as a driver of change is the independent appraisal of the conditions that have been inherited. In the words of Popper:

> *There can be no history of 'the past as it actually did happen'; there can only be interpretations, and none of them final; and every generation has a right to frame its own...not only...a right..., it also has a kind of obligation to do so; for there is indeed a pressing need to be answered. We want to know how our troubles are related to the past, and we want to see the line along which we may progress towards the solution of what we feel, and what we choose, to be our main tasks.*
>
> (Popper, 1966, Vol. 2: 268)

Since time immemorial, 'education' has been understood as having dual aims:

- One set of aims may be summarised as instrumental rather than intrinsic, concerned with cultural transmission, training and social control. This aspect of education is concerned with transmitting cultural norms, expectations and values from one generation to the next; preparing people to occupy their destined roles within society; and giving them occupational skills intended to match the perceived future economic needs of the community.
- The other set of aims may be summarised as emphasising education's intrinsic value, concerned with enabling each individual to blossom to their full potential. This aspect of education is concerned with empowerment: with equipping people with the skills and knowledge that will enable them to take control of their own future, including their own future learning. Central to this aim is enabling an individual to reach the full potential of their aptitudes, to be creative, to think critically, to develop fresh ideas and to move thinking forwards.

These two aims (or emphases, since in practice education must address the first aim to some extent) represent markedly different standpoints. In the first, the education system is saying to pupils, 'We know what the future will bring, and the future belongs to us. We know what role you will have in that future, and we know the knowledge and skills you will need in order to meet the expectations surrounding that role. We will transmit to you that knowledge and those skills. (And if you have a problem with that, you are "disaffected").'

In the second, the education system is saying to pupils, 'We do not know what the future will bring, and that future will belong to you, not to us. We do not know what your roles will be or where life will take you – the possibilities are almost endless. Our knowledge will be replaced by new knowledge. Our job is to enable you to develop the skills, confidence and beliefs to make the very best of yourself and your opportunities, and to play your part in developing different and better futures for society.'

This dichotomy is similar to that drawn by Popper between closed and open societies:

> The magical or tribal or collectivist society will also be called the closed society, *and the society in which individuals are confronted with personal decisions, the* open society.

> (Popper, 1966, Vol. 1: 173)

A moral commitment to the empowering purposes of education is paralleled, somewhat bleakly, in Popper's advocacy of the open society:

If we are tempted to rely on others...if we shrink from the task of...
reason, of responsibility...we must try to fortify ourselves with a clear
understanding of the simple decision before us. We can return to the
beasts. But if we wish to remain human, then there is only one way,
the way into the open society...using what reason we may have to
plan as well as we can for both security and freedom.

(Popper, 1966, Vol. 1: 201)

The empowering aim for education is logically connected with particular standpoints on a whole range of educational issues, especially stances towards school staff and school students. Those in leadership positions in schools who subscribe to the aims of educative empowerment are likely to believe in the importance of modelling: the need for all of the adults working in a school to exemplify the attitudes and behaviours they advocate, and for the organisational life of the school to be conducted as far as possible in ways which are compatible with educational aims. If school leaders encourage a love of learning, they will want staff at all levels to demonstrate their own love of learning, seeing themselves primarily as learners, implying a strong culture of professional development. This approach is consistent with the concept of teaching as an evidence-informed profession, which emphasises the status of the teacher as a self-motivated professional, using action research and other problem-solving methods to refine continually the practical skills of teaching. The encouragement of reflective practice and practitioner research can be seen as both an indicator of commitment to education for empowerment, and as one of the tools for effecting its promotion.

Similarly, school leaders who are committed to the empowering aims of education are likely to believe strongly that pupils and students should be related to as partners in the process of learning. This view attaches importance to the fostering of mutual respect, cultivated by adults showing respect for children and young people as individuals who have rights, who should be listened to and taken seriously, and whose ideas and perceptions can contribute much to the development of a school climate conducive to learning. The 'conversations' introduced by Collarbone (1997), which engaged students in the process of 'turning around' a school, provided an early example of contemporary understandings of student voice and student agency. One of the most striking features in the case study of Sweyne Park School (see Appendix 2) is the strong and conscious connection between promoting research engagement and promoting high levels of student empowerment.

In Figure 8.1 the two dimensions of professional empowerment of staff and educative empowerment of students are used to propose a fourfold typology of schools.

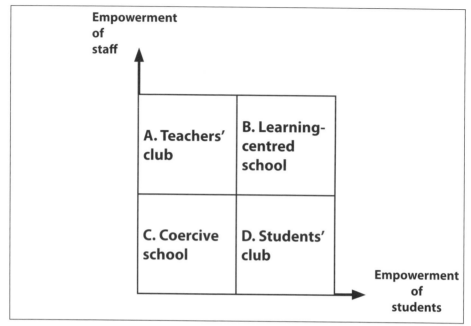

Figure 8.1 A typology of schools

Low empowerment of staff and students

If neither staff nor students experience very much empowerment as a result of their engagement with the organisation, the relationships between adults and students are likely to be confrontational and lacking in mutual respect, or of a calculating, transactional nature. In this climate, many students develop long-lasting negative sentiments towards formal learning. Staff morale is likely to be low and turnover high; they feel unsupported. These conditions might be found in a school facing challenging circumstances or under intervention; they might also be found where the school's management has been static for a long period and has not adapted to changing needs, or is unusually autocratic. The label 'Coercive school' is attached to this category.

High staff empowerment, low student empowerment

It is possible in certain situations for a school to develop a professional culture which gives staff high levels of empowerment that are not shared by the students. Some very traditional, academic schools may give teachers high status and considerable freedom in how they approach their work, but require rigid conformity from their students. Or a school might be in challenging circumstances but use certain kinds of staff development and engagement in off-site projects as a form of relief, and as a distraction from addressing the harsh realities of the students' immediate needs, affording the students no equivalent reliefs or distractions. The label 'Teachers' club' is attached to this category.

Low staff empowerment, high student empowerment

In other schools, the position may be reversed, so that the students receive high levels of empowerment while the staff do not. These situations are rare. They can arise, for example, in some independent international schools, where there is an unusually assertive (and perhaps wealthy) body of parents who encourage their children to be equally assertive, and who receive the backing of the headteacher or proprietor of the school, in which teachers have low status and have to do as they are told. In this example, the empowerment of the students cannot necessarily be regarded as educative empowerment. Another example might arise where the leadership of a school is determined to engage the students as change agents, perhaps seeing this as the only way of forcing staff to accept that there are issues to be addressed. Here, the imbalance between empowerment of students and staff would be a temporary phase in a process of development. The label 'Students' club' is applied to this category.

High empowerment of staff and students

Some schools achieve high levels of empowerment both of staff and students. This is likely to be the result of a clear educational vision. These schools will have a positive and developmental professional culture, well-developed strategies for teaching and learning, relationships of mutual respect between staff and students, concern for the students' 'total experience' of the school, and encouragement of a productive interface between the school and students' families. The label 'Learning-centred school' can justly be attached to this category.

Some schools may be in a stable condition, residing for many years in the same position on Figure 8.1. Other schools may be in a process of movement. Not all such movements are necessarily in a positive direction (for example a change of leadership may introduce a period of regression to 'coercive' characteristics). Many schools will be engaged in a journey towards higher levels of empowerment of staff and students. That journey is unlikely to be represented by a single straight line. Some schools may regard it as essential to concentrate in the first instance on developing the professional culture of the staff, as shown in Figure 8.2.

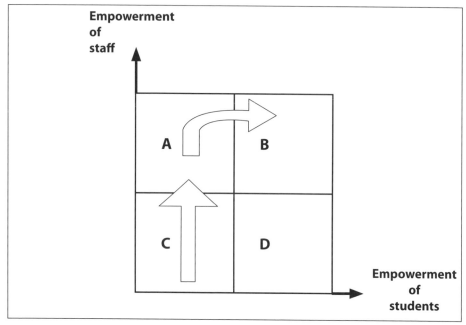

Figure 8.2 Teachers as agents of change

In other situations, a choice may be made to pursue the hazardous strategy of giving priority to student empowerment, as shown in Figure 8.3.

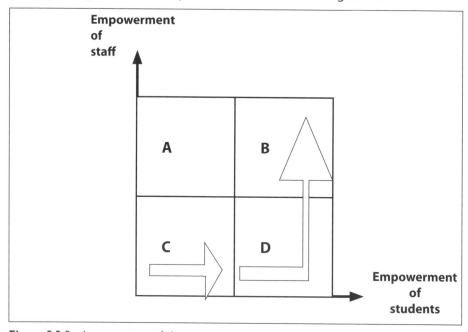

Figure 8.3 Students as agents of change

Many schools take a twin-track approach: a series of concurrent initiatives to empower staff and to empower students, stimulating learning and generating new working relationships. This combination of strategies is represented in Figure 8.4. It is evident at the schools of Edwin and Sonia (and partially at the schools of the other leaders) described in Chapter 4 and in the case study of Sweyne Park School described in Appendix 2.

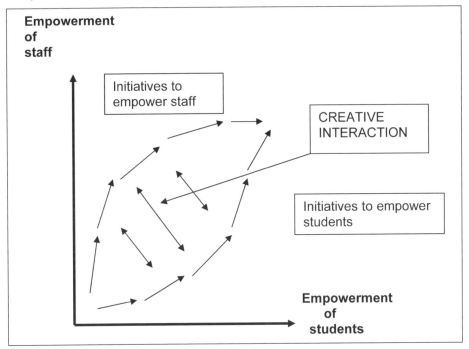

Figure 8.4 All are agents of change

Research engagement and school culture

The ideas shared in the section above have been derived naturalistically: by looking at schools where research engagement has been taken seriously over an extended period; by listening to the educational thinking of research-engaged headteachers; and by taking note of the kinds of initiatives to which they have given priority. Of course it is the case that there will be schools exhibiting the same pattern of development which have used methods other than research engagement to achieve their learning-centredness. This book avoids claiming causal relationships between the practice of research engagement and the achievement of any specific school development outcome. Any implication of exclusivity – of research engagement being the *only* route to particular benefits – must be rejected even more strongly, as it could so easily be falsified by finding contrary instances. There is, nonetheless, a definite alignment and compatibility between the kinds of thinking that value research engagement, including practitioner research, and the kinds of thinking that see the educative empowerment of staff and students as appropriate vehicles to use on the school development journey.

It is also the case that once educative empowerment of staff and students has become a chosen strategy for school development, research engagement offers a strikingly strong suite of tactics for giving effect to that strategy. 'Knowledge is power': to be effective, student voice needs to be backed by data. 'Voice' progresses to students sharing core issues of school leadership (i.e. the leadership of learning), when they are enabled to generate and own data, and to be confident in interacting with it critically to feed a sophisticated level of debate. Initiatives which promote the development of students as researchers are clearly supportive of the development of student voice and leadership. In the same way, the professional empowerment of staff has to be fed by information and knowledge, which are owned by the staff (whether individually or collectively) and which may be subjected to critical commentary. This condition is met where staff are able to generate their own information and knowledge through practitioner research and where, on their own initiative, they access the products of externally generated research.

The development of 'learning-centredness' through empowered and informed dialogue, as illustrated in Figure 8.1, is dependent upon acceptance of a range of viewpoints and opinions, otherwise the parties to the dialogue might just as well talk to themselves. This acceptance is not one of resigned tolerance ('we have to work with these people'), but one which recognises the fact of increasing diversity within most communities and organisations, and the contested nature of much officially promulgated articulation of school improvement matters. Stewart Ranson has identified the interrelationships between dialogue embracing diversity, the 'learning society' and the ability of communities to cope with future conditions:

> It is only when the values and processes of learning are placed at the centre of the polity that the conditions can be established for all individuals to develop their capacities, and that institutions can respond openly and imaginatively to a period of change.
>
> (Ranson, 1998: 101)

Ranson's understanding of the 'learning society' is closely complementary both to Fullan's 'moral purpose' (Fullan, 1993) and to Popper's 'open society' (Popper, 1966). The following two paragraphs summarise Ranson's central line of argument.

In the learning society, learning is accepted as the key to future well-being and is placed at the centre of experience. Learning is the powerful process which helps an individual to develop the skills and capacities to respond imaginatively to change, to shape their own future and to understand better the processes both of change and of learning. The learning society is, therefore, characterised by a self-sustaining beneficial cycle of experience and reflexivity, in which coping with change deepens the capacity to cope with further change. The kind of learning involved concentrates on fundamental learning skills and attitudes, including the learner's ability to take the initiative; it is conscious, largely informal, lifelong and can only be achieved through dialogue with others, rather than in isolation.

The learning society recognises diversity and regards the differences between communities as a source of strength. Different groups learn to communicate with each other, and to understand the conflicting perceptions shaping society. Through reasoned public discourse in a spirit of tolerance, reflection and imagination, the learning society becomes receptive to others, more questioning of its own beliefs, less defensive and freer to take risks (Ranson, 1994, 1998).

There are clear parallels between the learning society thus described and the organisational culture cultivated in research-engaged schools. One dimension of this culture is the nature of the dialogues that are permitted and encouraged. Whose stories get told and listened to? Within what range is it seen as acceptable for individual professionals to articulate their educational thinking? Whose views matter most, and how closely does that mirror hierarchical seniority? The answers to these questions distinguish true collegiality from pseudo-discussions that are simply a technique used by management to impose its will.

Agendas of school improvement

The discussion above emphasised the dynamic nature of the school development journey in relation to the factor of empowerment of staff and students, and suggested conceptual resonances between that journey and interest in research engagement. The active promotion of school research engagement may be a contributory motive for wanting higher levels of staff and student empowerment; it will also contribute as a means of bringing about that change; and it can, to some extent, serve also as an indicator that the desired level of empowerment is really happening.

As noted, an important expression of 'empowerment' is the nature and quality of the dialogues that are supported. The dynamic condition of schools leads on to a consideration of the different points that schools have reached on their journey of development, and how that might affect their approach to research engagement. The introduction of this factor is used to speculate about the patterns of research engagement that might, on the basis of deduction, be seen as practicable by a hypothetical school developing from intervention to stability, and then on to a system leadership role.

When a school is failing, requiring intervention and 'turnaround', the concerns of leadership are short term. They need to demonstrate to external stakeholders that key issues (usually concerning teaching and learning) are being addressed. Staff are likely to be demotivated, lacking confidence in their own abilities, highly risk-averse and fearful of interim managements that may be perceived as wanting to apportion blame. Dialogues are likely to be strictly curtailed, with an emphasis on achieving conformity to the leader's requirements. These conditions are extremely hostile to the fostering of engagement in practitioner research of the conventional kind. The school leadership may, however, be thirsty for certain kinds of data, including quantitative analysis of attainment, reports of lesson observations and the views of students. There may also be a desire for any suitably robust information indicating a strength of the school or progress that has been made by the new regime. Insofar as the leadership is applying evidence-based practice, the research evidence (for example on effective interventions) is likely to be accessed in indirect and highly processed forms, such as through the guidance of school improvement agencies.

The strategies which typify intervention and 'turnaround' are associated with the effective schools movement, including a preference for the top-down imposition of 'proven' solutions. Numerous writers emphasise the desirability and value to school leadership approaches during this phase of cultivating the empowerment of staff – see, for example, Crow (2005), Stoll *et al.* (2001) and Turner (1998) – but in reality the scales may often be weighted against this.

Rea and Weiner described the position thus:

> *The seemingly genuine wish to empower teaching professionals masks the range of macro- and micro-political features of managerialism... which militate against such empowerment...If prescriptions are adhered to, the promise is that the individual or institution will be 'empowered' to change. The change required, however...is a reflection... of wider political...interests. Change thus becomes bureaucratic and managerial, administered through development plans, programmes, targets, outputs and measures of success and failure.*
>
> (Rea and Weiner, 1998: 27)

When a school reaches the stage of fragile recovery, the concerns of leadership will continue to be short term but also increasingly medium term.

There will be a need to sustain the trajectory of improvement following the initial acute interventions. Staff are likely to be regaining confidence, but if leaders do not evolve their style to suit the circumstances, the staff may be resentful of the prolongation of top-down managerialism. If the leadership is sympathetic to research engagement, at this stage there may be some support for practitioner research projects as part of a suite of improvement strategies. This is likely to be a controlled process, with areas of investigation focusing on school improvement priorities, and with projects being related to individuals' performance management objectives. It is to be hoped that by this stage professional dialogues will be more two-way, relaxed and inclusive, but the leadership will be wary of staff pursuing lines of enquiry that might distract their attention from immediate priorities. A school at this stage of development is able to give more attention to published research findings in the fields most closely related to its priorities.

At the stage of stable achievement, a school's concerns give more attention to the longer term, for example the strategic trajectory of the school's development and where it plans to position itself in the future. The school is in a position to take a more strategic approach to staff development, perhaps supporting cohorts of staff in undertaking further study, including practitioner research projects. The pattern of the school's external relations, previously dominated by intervention agencies, will have broadened to give greater attention to lateral partnerships. The leadership style will give greater emphasis to capacity-building and collegiality, and this will be reflected in the quality of professional dialogue. A school at this stage of development is ideally placed to become research-engaged, both through strategic support for practitioner research, and through active engagement with published research findings.

The highest stage of development is when a school has established a strong and secure reputation for excellence, and is offering school system leadership by supporting other schools. The concerns of leadership include maintaining and increasing reputation for excellence: 'staying at the top of the greasy pole'. The school largely 'runs itself', is able to attract and retain excellent staff, and – with senior leaders heavily involved in external engagements – is enabling others to gain more leadership responsibility. The school has sufficient reputational capital to be able to pioneer innovations involving risk and which may not offer pay-back in the short term. According to the interests of the school's leadership, excellence in research engagement may be one of the dimensions of system leadership. Professional dialogues will be sophisticated and extending beyond the school, for example by contributing to significant conferences. Schools at this stage have the capacity to exemplify the highest levels of research engagement, including contributing to the growth of practitioner knowledge through publications and influencing policy.

Agendas of social justice and equity

Many fields of research are closely interrelated with agendas of social and political change. Some conceptual lenses through which research may be undertaken, perhaps most notably Marxist and feminist perspectives, have resulted in the generation of new meta-narratives: new overarching ways of understanding history and what is going on in the world. Research of this kind challenges people to review their basic assumptions: a previously held understanding of 'the facts of the matter' is exposed to be merely one chosen interpretation – an interpretation, moreover, that may serve the interests of one group and be detrimental to others.

Across a wide range of fields, covering many topics and issues, research is undertaken not just with a view to putting forward new understandings, but also for the purpose of supporting actual processes of change. Generally, researchers do what they do because they believe it will help to make the world a better place, whether the aim is improving the efficiency of a technical process or advancing the interests of a particular group within society. This aim is seen particularly clearly in research in the fields of social justice and equity. But in selecting that perhaps too easy example, it is important to remember that most educational research – whether overtly or not, whether self-consciously or not – is supporting one cause or another.

Morwenna Griffiths' book *Educational Research for Social Justice* is subtitled *Getting off the fence* (Griffiths, 1998). This is a book 'about taking sides and getting change in education through educational research' (p.3). Griffiths described a range of positions that could be held on the relationship between facts and values. At one extreme is the view that facts are value-free, and that researchers can, therefore, simply research facts without needing to consider values. A middle position is that research will always be biased by value judgements, but the aim of the researcher should be to minimise this effect. At the other end of the spectrum is the view that facts and information are necessarily value-laden, but it is unhelpful to use the term 'bias', because this implies the possibility of a neutral view. From this position, it is preferable for the researcher to identify their perspective and to state it openly. This position also acknowledges the human aspect of education and education research, where 'facts' are largely interpretations, affected by human agency and self-understanding (Griffiths, 1998: 46).

This position accords with that of Popper on the subjectivity of enquiry:

Where I am explaining my personal proposals or decisions in moral and political matters, I have always made the personal character of the proposal or decision clear. It rather means that the selection of the subject matter treated is a matter of personal choice to a much greater extent than it would be, say, in a scientific treatise. In a way, however, this difference is a matter of degree. Even a science is not merely a 'body of facts'. It is, at the very least, a collection, and as such it is dependent upon the collector's interests, upon a point of view.

(Popper, 1966, Vol. 2: 259)

All description is selective…a mere selection, and a small one at that, of the facts that present themselves for description…It is not only impossible to avoid a selective point of view, but also wholly undesirable to attempt to do so…a point of view is inevitable; and the naïve attempt to avoid it can only lead to self-deception, and to the uncritical application of an unconscious point of view.

(Popper, 1966, Vol. 2: 261)

The view might reasonably be taken that Griffiths's third position applies widely within educational research, and especially within practitioner research: the researcher has aims and purposes to which they expect their research to contribute, and on that matter they do not falsely seek or claim neutrality. That said, the nature of the positions taken by researchers can be unpacked a little.

In the context of debate about feminism within educational research, Michelle Fine noted that some researchers position themselves as participatory activists, researching in order to 'unearth, disrupt and transform existing ideological and/or institutional arrangements' (Fine, 1994: 17). She identified three stances: 'ventriloquy', 'voices' and 'activism'. 'Ventriloquy' involves words and ideas that are really the author's own appearing to come from another source; the subjects of the research tell 'truths' for which the researcher does not need to accept responsibility:

Ventriloquy…can be found in all research narratives in which the researchers' privileges and interests are camouflaged. Ventriloquy means…treating subjects as objects while calling them subjects. And ventriloquy requires the denial of all politics in the very political work of social research.

(Fine, 1994: 19)

The stance of 'voices' is slightly different in that it involves the reporting of authentic voices from particular groups, but the choice of the group ensures that the material presented will support a particular 'cause':

Scholars – critical ethnographers in particular – have used voices to accomplish a subtler form of ventriloquism. While such researchers appear to let the 'Other' speak, just under the covers of those marginal, if now 'liberated' voices, we hide…Voices offer a qualitative opportunity for scholars interested in generating critical, counter-

hegemonic analyses of institutional arrangements...Through such work, many of us have been fortunate. We've collected rich and multi-situated voices from adolescents – dropouts in my case... It's consistently easy to gather up their stories of critique, dissent, contradictory consciousness...in order to tell a story.

(Fine, 1994: 19–20)

Griffiths (1998) explored in some depth the relationship between voice and empowerment through the research process, and drew attention to the issues of how researchers use the voices captured from the group they are researching, and whether and how that differs between researchers who are 'insiders' or 'outsiders' in relation to the group concerned (Griffiths, 1998: Chapter 8). One of the debates in writing in this field is, for example, whether, and with what provisos, it is possible for white researchers to analyse and interpret the voice of black research subjects.

Fine's third stance was activism:

Participatory activist research...assumes that knowledge is best gathered in the midst of social change projects; that the partial perspectives of participants and observers can be collected by researchers in 'power sensitive conversations' which need to be transformative...This work is, at once: disruptive, transformative and reflective; about understanding and about action; not about freezing the scene but always about change…Scholarship on school reform, racism, community life, violence against women, reproductive freedom, sits at the messy nexus of theory, research and organising. The raison d'être *for such research is to unsettle questions, texts and collective struggles; to challenge what is, incite what could be, and help imagine a world that is not yet imagined. Done critically... this work trespasses borders of class, ethnicities, sexualities, genders and politics.*

(Fine,1994: 28–9, 30)

Griffiths (1998) identified three categories of 'research for social justice'. The first is research that is focused directly on the justice issue, such as studies where the central topic is, for example, provision for children with special educational needs, or the achievement of ethnic minority pupils. Her second category is research where the central topic is about something other than social justice issues, such as school organisation or teachers' professional development, but the research is undertaken from a positioned standpoint so that the social justice issues are in fact addressed in the context of a more general study. The third category is research in which the methodologies and epistemologies used are themselves the factors that advance a positioned agenda (Griffiths, 1998: 26).

These positioned research agendas need to be on the radar of school leaders promoting research engagement. Their own stances and positioning would be best thought through in advance:

- How will they react if a keen member of staff wants to do what Fine (1994) described as 'gathering partial perspectives' with the specific intention to be 'disruptive, transformative, inciting what could be'?
- To what extent should the school sanction research activity that will analyse it through the lenses of oppression and struggle?
- Is it appropriate for school staff to encourage the expression and gathering of viewpoints with the prior knowledge that these will be controversial and perhaps divisive?

The answers to these questions are not straightforward. Enlightened leaders serving a community of diversity and disadvantage may see activist research as aligned with their moral purpose, and working through the issues as a price worth paying for necessary reform. The extent and nature of positioning in research may not become apparent until after resources have been committed and permissions given. Where the research forms part of an accredited university course, there can be a grey area within which the researcher may claim that they should be embraced within the university's policies regarding academic freedom. Different considerations arise where the researchers are students rather than staff.

In all cases, reasonable balances have to be struck, and school leaders must be wary of classifying issues as being about research that might be better seen as matters of ordinary school management.

Agendas of innovation

The sections above have explored the agendas for school research engagement that arise from views about the aims and purposes of education, approaches to school development, and the positioned stance of the work and literatures produced within particular fields of research. To complete the picture, it is necessary to note also two cross-cutting themes: innovation and globalisation.

One the one hand, innovation may include finding new and better ways to meet an existing need, or adapting known methods to meet a new need, or developing new methods to meet a new need. These elements are not as distinct as they appear, because an innovative cast of mind helps to shape what is seen as a 'need'. Some of the issues regarded as pressing by educators today are not new – they were simply not regarded as problematical by previous generations, who had different expectations for the outcomes of schooling. Worthwhile innovation, to meet an identified need, should be distinguished from innovation for its own sake, and from self-designated 'innovation' which, upon examination, is not innovatory at all. Both of these, when practised by senior leaders, may be motivated by attention-seeking and career advancement, or to distract attention from weaknesses elsewhere in their work.

On the other hand, at the micro-level of individual teachers undertaking action research, the spirit of innovation is intrinsic to the methodology, which includes cycles of experimentation and review. The sense of undertaking that journey of discovery is one of the motivations and sources of satisfaction associated with practitioner research. The new practices developed through the cycles of action research in most cases will not be new to the world, but will be new to that individual in that context, so it would seem mean-spirited to deny the attachment of the term 'innovation' to such work.

On a larger scale, developments in the technologies of learning, including ICT, have offered major opportunities for innovation in the range of tools and resources available to support educators in their work. These have impacted on the curriculum, on teaching and learning methods, on assessment and on school management. Phases of development have been directly related to the march of technology: from computer rooms with ICT lessons, to 'laptop for every child' policies, to hand-held devices, to intranets, interactive whiteboards, and so on. For the research-engaged school, ICT has transformed: the scale and intensity of communication; access to research findings; the capacity to undertake in-school research projects; and the capacity to engage students as researchers. How to increase the effective use of ICT is also an ideal and popular subject for practitioner enquiry.

The agenda of innovation as motivation for practitioner research might most readily be associated with the use of educational ICT. Looking into the future, that view may be valid, especially in relation to educational development on a global scale, but a historical perspective points to different conclusions. Suppose one were to stand in the preserved nineteenth-century schoolhouse in the Beamish Museum in County Durham, England, and to ask: 'What educational innovations have made the biggest differences to children's lives?'. What are the most profound changes from that time to the kind of education offered in a modern school, which may still be using a building of the same age?

First impressions may well point to the transformation of the learning environment and its technologies. In the nineteenth-century schoolhouse, walls and décor are dark brown instead of modern pale or bright colours; children sit at monastic style desks ('forms') rather than at modern flexible furniture; writing slate has now been replaced by exercise books and computers; wall posters and a globe have been replaced by internet resources. Yet these changes, while striking, are not the most profound. The mass education introduced in nineteenth-century England was to keep the labouring classes in their place: to teach the children of the labouring classes to accept their position in life, to respect their betters, and to learn the skills that would make them useful in the menial occupations to which they were destined (see, for example, Carr and Hartnett, 1996).

Modern schools have aspirational aims for their students, wanting them to have broad horizons and to escape the limitations of their origins. In the nineteenth-century schoolhouse, order was maintained through fear and the frequent and brutal use of physical punishment. Modern schools concern themselves with their students' well-being and respect their human rights, dignity and individuality. The case may well be argued that innovations in the aims and purposes of schooling, and in the quality and nature of interpersonal relationships in school, have had even more profound benefit to children's lives than innovations in the technologies of learning. Practitioner research projects in fields such as the development of student voice, or measures to overcome the attainment gap between children of low and high socio-economic backgrounds, may be seen as contributing to this innovatory agenda.

Agendas of globalisation

The subject of globalisation is linked to that of innovation, because 'globalisation' as usually understood is a consequence of innovations in technology, especially ICT, and innovations in business, especially the global-scale management of capital and labour, and also of intellectual capital and corporate cultures.

Burbules and Torres (2000) questioned the inevitability of globalisation with respect both to its speed and to the differentiated patterns of its impact. It is helpful to distinguish between 'globalisation' as a top-down driver of changes, and as a bottom-up outcome of changes. In both cases, its effects include mixtures of benefits and disadvantages, which will differ between different groups within society. From the top-down perspective, globalisation can be understood as an unstoppable force with its own momentum, to which people at the local level adapt as best they can. From the bottom-up perspective, the trends known as 'globalisation' are the cumulative outcome of many decisions made by individuals, corporations and governments. Paraphrasing Popper, this perspective replaces the fatalism and passivity of historicism (Popper, 1966) with the proactivity of individual and collective responsibility to create the best future we can.

School leaders have to balance three sets of demands that may often be in tension with each other:

- the demands of governments and national expectations
- the obligations of their own professional knowledge
- the needs and aspirations of the local communities they serve.

The need to perform this balancing act applies to school leadership in general in the UK, before taking account of globalisation. These three sources of demand and the factors underlying them do, however, offer a key to making sense of 'globalisation' as it affects the operating contexts of schools.

First, global issues and developments are one of the factors shaping national policies and expectations, including what is seen as problematical, and what would 'count' as satisfactory 'solutions'.

Second, there are also global influences on professional educational knowledge and practice.

Third, the needs and aspirations presented to the school by the community it serves are greatly affected by the impacts of elements of globalisation, including impacts on the state of the local economy and labour market; on the ethnic, religious and socio-economic profiles of the community; and on its multi-layered patterns of cultural identity and affinity.

The factor of most relevance to a book like this about research engagement is that of professional knowledge, and the ways in which globalisation is impacting on the thinking and practice of school leaders and other school practitioners. A combination of easy internet access to information on educational developments around the world, participation in international conferences and international professional development opportunities, and an English language literature of school leadership that draws upon ideas and experiences from across the English-speaking world, has enabled school leaders (who choose to do so) to identify themselves with professional networks and patterns of thinking that, if not exactly global, are certainly international.

At the same time, officially encouraged initiatives have supported international school-to-school links that broaden students' experiences both through virtual links and actual exchange visits. There is clearly great potential for these international orientations to engender, and to be enhanced by, aspects of research engagement. For example, one of the strands of the UK-India Education and Research Initiative involved support for partnership linkages between schools in England and India that include both exchange visits for staff and students, and a series of action research projects (UKIERI, 2010). Schools engaged in international partnerships can also consider research findings on effective partnership practices, for example the study by Edge *et al.* (2009) of North–South school partnerships.

Conclusion

So, there are many legitimate – but different – agendas being pursued at every level: in the systemic support for school research engagement; among research-engaged schools as institutions; and in the minds of research-engaged individuals within them.

Readers will have their own perceptions of the extent to which, and pace at which, the teaching profession and the school system may develop further the inclination and means to practise the discourse, tolerance of diversity, reflection and imagination of Ranson's learning society, in which many agendas may co-exist through constructive dialogue (Ranson, 1998). To paraphrase Popper, it is for each individual to choose whether they will make it their purpose to support the open society.

This book opened with the assertion that 'knowledge is power'. Its chapters have explored how the knowledge derived from educational research can increase the power of school practitioners and leaders to influence their situations and to work towards their objective. This final chapter points towards a further assertion: that knowledge *about* knowledge can engender an even greater sense of professional empowerment. This kind of knowledge increases awareness of the agendas, stances, issues and movements behind the generation of information. Without that, the mass of 'evidence' available to schools can seem as overwhelming as stars on a clear night. Knowledge about knowledge provides insights comparable to the astronomer's arts, foregrounding the patterns which assist navigation.

Designing small-scale projects and investigations

This appendix to Chapter 5 offers guidance on designing and conducting small-scale projects and investigations. It is concerned with projects, usually using action research methodology, which involve practitioners in undertaking developments or investigations 'for real' in their work situation, and then reflecting on what they have learnt from this activity.

Effective action research benefits from:

- senior management support
- topic foci related to actual work priorities
- an in-school peer group
- realistic scoping
- robust arrangements for data capture and recording at every stage
- external support
- worthwhile dissemination
- being an ongoing process, part of how the organisation works.

The following are some of the factors to bear in mind when designing these projects:

- **Time:** If the project forms part of a higher degree programme, look at the programme schedule and see when the report of the project is to be submitted. Often this will be measured in weeks rather than months. Be realistic about what can be achieved in the given time. This is one assignment, not a life's work!
- **Scope:** A project that is precisely defined and treats one issue thoroughly is usually better than one which ranges widely and superficially across too broad a field.
- **Clear research question:** Within the chosen topic it is important to identify a specific research question (or group of questions) and that this/these continue to be refined as the work proceeds.

- **Relevance to work:** It is always advisable to pick projects that are relevant to current work priorities, so that there is a clear point to the project and other people will be less likely to question why the activity is taking place. For the researcher, this minimises the amount of extra time they need to invest in the programme, because much of the work involved in the project would have to be undertaken in any case.
- **Control:** All other factors being equal, it is less risky to choose a project that can be delivered largely within the control of the researcher and their immediate colleagues. Projects heavily dependent on the actions and voluntary co-operation of a wider range of colleagues are more difficult to control and more likely to fall behind schedule.
- **Official support:** Generally, projects are more secure where they have clear official support, such as where they contribute to an action in the school development plan or receive official and public endorsement from senior management.

Reading

Reading is an important component of any practitioner research project. It is essential to relate the actions and reflections undertaken to published ideas and research findings. Those sources also help practitioner researchers to understand the nature and causes of the 'problems' they intend to tackle through their projects, and to make informed choices about the intervention strategies used.

The literature also provides a common language for describing and discussing the issues, events, behaviours and other phenomena observed:

- **Be realistic about how much it is possible to read:** It is better to identify and read texts that are widely referenced ('seminal') and just a few others, with real understanding and application, than to attempt to cover too wide a range of sources.
- **Read purposefully:** Do not simply open a text and read it like a novel, hoping that this will somehow 'do you good'. A quick initial skim should help you to judge what you are likely to gain from the reading. It might spark off ideas for a suitable project, or elaborate some of the concepts you are working with, or enable you to consider how the 'findings' presented in an article relate to your own institution, or provide a method of explaining things you have observed.
- **Read critically:** Writers are mainly expressing opinions, not facts. Writers' underlying beliefs may not always be stated overtly. Where is this particular writer 'coming from'? What assumptions do they seem

to be making? Do you agree with their viewpoint? Do they say things which grate against your own beliefs and values?

Reflecting

'Reflecting' in the context of 'reflective practice' can take various forms. The following are four of its main components:

- **Develop a dual perspective:** A reflective practitioner must be able to move to and fro between two states of mind: being part of the action, wholly engaged as a player, influencing and being influenced along with everyone else; and then periodically stepping back to be a detached observer, looking with cool neutrality at what is going on.
- **Engage in structured self-evaluation and review:** Everyone knows (by how they feel) whether they have had a good or bad day, but a reflective practitioner will 'unpack', analyse and articulate those feelings (to themselves) in a way that is structured, systematic, and leads to positive future developments.
- **Use theory to understand work issues:** Reflection involves drawing upon the ideas and concepts presented in books and articles to develop a deeper understanding of day-to-day professional practice, and to develop and deepen a coherent set of personal beliefs about these matters.
- **Conscious learning:** Everyone learns through living, but much of that learning is unconscious and may include much that is negative or limiting. Reflective practitioners are people who are not only actively open to learning, but who are also more conscious of the processes of their own learning, and more able to use that learning to address the issues in their lives and work.

Observing ethical standards

Judyth Sachs used the notion of 'ethical literacy' in relation to school-based practitioner researchers who are not steeped in the thinking of research ethics (Sachs, 2007: xiv). Increasing ethical literacy may be a professional development need.

Practitioner research involves writing down accounts of projects undertaken in school, and reflections on them. This often involves directly or indirectly expressing opinions about the work of colleagues. It also involves critical enquiry and independent thinking of a kind which some people might interpret as criticism of the school. As noted earlier, the ethical issues are complex and it is important to be aware of the BERA guidelines. The following are some absolute basics:

- Make sure that someone in the school, such as the headteacher or your in-school mentor, knows what projects or investigations you are undertaking. Check that they are, in general, happy with them. Discuss potentially sensitive issues with this person before going ahead.
- Ask yourself to what extent the project you intend to undertake is an integral part of your normal job. If that is completely the case, the processes, protocols and courtesies to observe will be predominantly those that apply to normal good working relations. If the project involves matters *which others might regard* as outside your normal core business, then it becomes more important to explain what you are doing and to ask relevant colleagues and students for their consent and co-operation.
- If you write down anything that could be perceived as critical of a colleague's work (even if they are not identifiable), then ask yourself: Do I have objective evidence to support this view? Have I discussed this with my mentor/supervisor/superior? Do I really need to include this in order to produce a complete and honest account? Would I be comfortable if I found the person concerned reading over my shoulder?

Increasing the validity of accounts

The following are ways in which to increase the validity of accounts of school-based projects:

- Conclusions drawn are clearly based on evidence, and the link between the evidence and the conclusion is clearly argued.
- Where appropriate, more than one method of data capture has been used.
- The account clearly distinguishes original data from analysis: 'Here are the facts. This is how I now interpret them.'
- Other people are involved in discussion at more than one of the key stages (project design, data capture, analysis, interpretation, conclusions), and this involvement is recorded in the account. In particular, conclusions have been tested out and are supported.

A case study of a research-engaged school: Sweyne Park School

Chapter 6 included a brief introduction to this case study, which illustrates a contemporary example of school leadership fostering the development of school research engagement.

Research engagement at Sweyne Park School, Rayleigh, Essex, is one component of an integrated school leadership approach that has proved highly successful; it cannot meaningfully be reported separately from the other components of the package.

Analogies engendered by the author in the course of conducting the case study included: the way a kite can only fly high because it is held by the string; or how each of the poles forming a tripod needs the counterbalancing support of the other two poles, while the poles of a tripod need some kind of cap or banding around the top to hold them in place. Without wishing to overwork the tripod analogy, the 'capping' at Sweyne Park was an unusually strong and shared commitment to the educative empowerment of the students, and the three 'poles' were research engagement, the school's involvement in initial teacher education, and the school's professional culture.

The culture was an outcome of low staff turnover combined with particular structures and systems for leadership, which were well embedded. At many schools, the headteacher is the device holding the 'poles' together, whereas here it seemed that the leadership had created a system with its own equilibrium, which would be sustainable if they walked away. There was also a truly symbiotic relationship between the trajectory of rising student attainment and the trajectory of research engagement. While undoubtedly the research engagement had contributed to successful outcomes, it was equally the case that the school (being so obviously successful in its primary purpose) created an environment within which research engagement was able to flourish.

Background

The school had been amalgamated from two schools with falling rolls in 1997. The headteacher at the time, Kate Spiller, adopted professional development and research engagement as the means to bring the two staffs together and to address the issues. She died in office in 2006, and her way of working was continued and built upon. For some schools, of which Sweyne Park is one, the story of their journey – and the legacy of a former leader honoured in memory – are profound influences on the school's culture, sense of direction and pride.

A few weeks before the case study visit, the school had received an 'outstanding' inspection grade from Ofsted, and the report had included the comment that the school had 'a culture of high expectations that staff and pupils support. The success of this is reflected in the willingness of all staff to improve their practice.'

Following the normal initial negotiations, the school provided some background information and proposed a list of staff to be interviewed. The merit of this arrangement was that it enabled the school's story to be listened to as told in its own way. The people who kindly gave their time to this were Andy Hodgkinson (Headteacher), Sally Pemberton (Deputy Headteacher), Corina Seal (Advanced Skills Teacher with responsibility for research engagement), Heather Hodgkinson (a former Assistant Headteacher employed for two half-days per week as Consultant supporting professional development), Ann Keogh (Head of Science), Nicole Paynter (Head of Maths), Gerry Seal (Data Manager) and David Wright (Newly Qualified Teacher (NQT) – Geography).

The interviews were mainly unstructured, except for occasional prompts and encouragements, in order to allow space for an element of grounded theory, and to keep the perceptions captured as near as possible to the authentic voices and interests of the participants, who make their own points clearly enough. In the sections that follow, the perceptions thus captured are interpreted through several analytical lenses:

- The overall framework within which to group representative comments is provided by the checklist for researcher-leadership introduced in Chapter 6, thereby illustrating the practical application of this instrument.
- Second, Chapter 1 offered three definitions of the research-engaged school: those of this author, those of Handscomb and MacBeath (2003) and those of Sharp *et al.* (2006a), against which this case study is measured.
- A further set of analytical lenses is taken from Middlewood *et al.* (1999), who researched a range of questions regarding the practice and impact of practitioner research through the experiences and contexts of participants in one particular higher degree programme.

Of particular relevance is Middlewood's exploration of the effects on staff and relationships of multiple research projects being undertaken in a school (Middlewood, in Middlewood *et al.*, 1999: Chapter 6). Summarising data drawn from a number of different schools, Middlewood identified as significant the development of staff as individual reflective practitioners – through professional reading, enhanced first-hand experience and knowledge, increased informal professional dialogue, and collaboration with colleagues. These aspects of individual growth were accompanied by new relationships with, and attitudes towards, the students. They were engendered by knowledge of the students obtained through investigations, by the process of involving students in research, and by the teachers' experience of themselves becoming students once again. These findings have direct parallels with this case study. Middlewood also explored the nature of senior management involvement, which presented a mixed picture, because in the schools studied, research engagement had not generally been initiated by the leadership, and for that reason those findings are less relevant (Middlewood, 1999).

The habit of professional reading, noted by Middlewood, was evident at Sweyne Park:

> *I found TLA [Teacher Learning Academy] a good process – it made me read books.*
>
> (Head of Science)

> *Sometimes we distribute research overviews. There is a staff library.*
>
> (Advanced Skills Teacher)

> *I use the staff reference library, and the Deputy Headteacher is very good in pointing towards other sources of information.*
>
> (NQT – Geography)

> *Next year I will look at esteem and confidence building with low achievers. I will do some personal reading using materials already identified, then test out some ideas and review them.*
>
> (Head of Maths)

Engagement of students

The enhanced significance given to the engagement of students, noted by Middlewood as a factor associated with school-based practitioner research, has already been identified as one of the striking features of Sweyne Park School:

We want the students to be more independent. We train most of the teachers so they are part of this culture. Other new teachers not trained here find it hard to adjust to the culture: our students are used to a sense of respect and engagement.

(Deputy Headteacher)

Student voice is huge. There are year councils and the school council, and a lot of work with Year 6–7 transition. For example, a geography project was 'Is this school a nice place?'. The students researched this question and some of their ideas will be put into practice.

(NQT – Geography)

I can see the benefits for students. Teaching doesn't become stagnant: we can always see new ways to encourage the students; we are always moving on and bringing the students with us.

(Head of Science)

We use consultants in connection with the professional development of staff in the department. It is a close group; sometimes they identify their needs more easily to an external person. The consultants interview pupils and this is fed back for professional development. We have a curriculum day for one subject for the whole day, and this development takes account of the interviews with pupils.

(Head of Maths)

In my TLA work I have been trying out new approaches to move away from a teacher-led classroom, introducing more pupil-led tasks, and finding out which groups these work best with.

(NQT – Geography)

These representative comments illustrate the depth and range of student engagement, which treats students' perceptions as of intrinsic importance, as well as providing feedback and contributing to decision-making.

School culture

In the study cited above, Middlewood (in Middlewood *et al.*, 1999: Chapter 7) also considered the influence of practitioner research on school culture, drawing particularly on the notion of the 'learning organisation' as developed by Aspinwall and Pedler (1997). He concluded that:

Widespread practitioners' in-house research can be a very powerful tool for influencing the development of the school culture to that of a learning organisation…The most significant factor (in managing this development)…may be the willingness and support of school leaders and senior managers to encourage such research in the first place.

(Middlewood, 1999: 101)

Aspinwall and Pedler had distinguished four types of learning, which could be summarised as knowledge, skills, personal development and collaborative achievement. They had also identified qualities of the learning school, which included: a commitment to lifelong learning for all those within the school; an emphasis on collaborative learning; a holistic understanding of the school as an organisation; and strong connections and relationships with the community and the world outside the school (Aspinwall and Pedler, 1997, cited in Middlewood, 1999; see also Pedler and Aspinwall, 1996, and Aspinwall, 1998).

Middlewood's findings were that all participants reported 'a growth in self-esteem achieved through the discovery process…and…a confidence that arises from authoritative first-hand knowledge', and the beneficial effects of professional reading, as examples of self-development (Middlewood, 1999: 107). Regarding collaborative learning:

They had found the support of the school group and the opportunity to work with others one of the most valuable and important factors in the success of the research programmes.

(Middlewood, 1999: 109)

In Middlewood's study, holistic understanding of the school as an organisation was represented by people understanding where they fitted into the whole picture, and how they were contributing to wider school developments. This understanding had caused them to become both more critical and more tolerant. He noted again that:

The increased awareness of the whole school included, for many teachers, a heightened consciousness of the centrality of students.

(Middlewood, 1999: 114)

Finally, Middlewood noted that organisational learning required critical awareness – an open and questioning attitude to the organisation itself.

It is clear that the organisational culture of Sweyne Park School displayed many points in common with those above, and in some ways perhaps took them even further. Distinctive features of the culture included low staff turnover, involvement in teacher training, emphasis on learning and collaboration, and use of the Teacher Learning Academy (TLA) scheme as one of the means to provide structures and systems for supporting professional learning. The following representative comments illustrate these points:

> *Sweyne Park School was formed when two schools with falling rolls joined together in 1997. The Headteacher was Kate Spiller, who had a particular interest in research and continuing professional development. I came to the school in 1997 as Assistant Headteacher working on staff training. We had to combine two staffs, and Kate Spiller's approach was to use staff development to achieve this. Research was always a strand, and we wanted involvement in initial teacher training so that we would have cutting-edge pedagogy. The IOE was involved in the 1999 batch, which brought new thinking in teaching and learning. We also had links with Cambridge and others. The impact was initially small: mainly CPD for the link person, but it made a statement about the school.*
>
> (Headteacher)

> *Staff retention is high. We have one of the lowest turnovers in Essex. Some teachers leave and then come back. We have a lot of teachers in their thirties, and have trained a lot of our own staff. This year we employed eight newly qualified teachers who had trained at the school.*
>
> (Deputy Headteacher)

> *The ethos of the school is that we are learners; for example, all NQTs complete a TLA presentation. Research is part of the job. It is not causing more work, because research is how to work more effectively for the students. A lot of staff stay a long time, so this approach has become embedded, because they have been surrounded by this culture. The school supports professional development. Staff joining without that background would probably be intimidated by it.*
>
> (Head of Maths)

> *All members of the department are involved in the TLA, they are enthusiastic. It is good, because it makes you think and gives new ideas. It is part of the school and the support is there.*
>
> (Head of Science)

> *The newly qualified teachers (NQTs) and people here taking initial teacher training get to try out this style of teaching and I have shared this work within the department as well as throughout and beyond the school. All department members have now done a TLA presentation*

on, for example, mentoring, lesson styles and assessment. Two are getting an MA in September from the Open University which includes a research project module. Another has just started.

(Head of Maths)

On the matter of critical awareness and openness to challenge, the following comment is significant:

The school doesn't suffer from arrogance – we are always looking to make things better.

(Data Manager)

Applying the checklist of researcher-leadership

The core of the case study information is presented through the framework of the checklist of researcher-leadership introduced in Chapter 6 (see Box 6.1). This is because the distinctive feature of research engagement at Sweyne Park is the way in which it has been nurtured by the school leadership over a long period. Inevitably, many of the comments captured could address more than one question, and some have been used in other sections of this account which would also have been helpful here. For these reasons, but also in reflection of the foci of interest expressed by the participants, the comments are spread unevenly across the sections of the checklist.

A. Inspiring

1. How and to what extent does the leadership team build and institutionalise a shared vision which is consistent with encouraging practitioner research?

Research engagement is part of the culture now. We take it for granted. It was introduced a few years ago and we were encouraged to go on courses and so on, but it is now self-sustaining.

(Head of Science)

2. How and to what extent does the leadership team encourage staff to develop their roles in ways which are conducive to practitioner research?

NQTs are really engaged. Some staff have plateaued. For some very experienced staff near retirement this is wonderful, for example, in the valuing of student voice, a lot of older teachers are thoroughly engaged.

(Advanced Skills Teacher)

The energy now comes from the teachers, who are finding new paths and ideas: they are now leading. It used to be towed by the Headteacher, leadership team, and heads of departments, but now the teachers are in the forefront and are leading.

(Deputy Headteacher)

We are always looking to develop teaching and learning one step ahead: it is a very thinking school, and the TLA allows each teacher to think of their own research.

(NQT – Geography)

This is definitely a research-based school with an emphasis on collaborative research. I started my research when as a head of department I identified a need for numeracy support. I wrote up a report (for the Gatsby Foundation) on the use of peer mentoring to engage younger pupils, and develop numeracy through play and games, which ran for two terms and which led to improvements in attitudes towards maths and confidence in class.

(Head of Maths)

I have also researched the impact of applying Kolb's theory within lessons, which has influenced my teaching style.

(Head of Maths)

I am given freedom in how I conduct the analysis of internal monitoring grades covering a full academic year which is sent to the relevant head of department and line manager in order to achieve identification and create actions regarding performance of various cohorts of pupils. I did a TLA on these analyses and expanded the system so that it was of interest to a greater number of departments. I make sure that all departments have a full set of data so that they can do their own research into the deviations from the averages for all departments. I expect all regular staff to understand these data, and I use them as a task for trainee teachers to interpret. Each head of department has a line manager. I analyse the data and send the line manager a set of questions they may wish to raise with the head of department.

(Data Manager)

The last comment above is interesting for a number of reasons. First, it is quantitatively based, which is unusual in practitioner enquiry, and bridges the assessment data management aspect of school life and the more familiar territory of the practitioner research movement. Second, it illustrates the strong infrastructure of line management and accountability and the way in which these draw upon and encourage research; research produces the questions which a line manager can use to challenge a head of department about learning outcomes, but part of that challenge is also to direct that department to the further investigations it needs to undertake.

Other points illustrated in these comments are the extent to which the leadership of research engagement has been institutionalised, and the strategic use of teacher training and the TLA as infrastructures supporting the processes of research engagement.

3. How and to what extent does the leadership team ensure that senior managers give support to staff who are engaged in practitioner research, and take interest in, and value, their findings?

There are three channels for CPD. In departments, it is run by the heads of department, who now see their role as including the leadership of CPD and research.

(Deputy Headteacher)

It is about the space you give people and the value you put on what people do. The leadership team gives the direction, so it isn't 'teacher-led reform'.

(Deputy Headteacher)

My work is now mostly to support the TLA activity. I work with staff, basically in a coaching role.

(Consultant)

We are all encouraged to take risks, try things out and make mistakes. If we try something that doesn't work, we don't worry about it. This culture comes through in all training sessions: we have them weekly in some form or other. This reflects the philosophy of the Headteacher and his predecessor, and is bought into by staff, which is why turnover is so low.

(Data Manager)

There is a strong line management and performance management system. The normal arrangement is one timetabled period with one's line manager weekly.

(Data Manager)

Significant points in these comments are: the way in which support for research engagement has been mainstreamed through the departmental structure and supported by strong line management; the acceptance of risk and giving of 'space'; and the provision of coaching support.

B. Social supporting

4. How and to what extent does the leadership team prioritise professional development in overall school development, giving it adequate resources, in ways which foster practitioner research?

Our 2001 Ofsted inspection went well. Tragically, in 2006, Kate Spiller who had started the research interest died, and I became Headteacher. The 2006 Ofsted report was very good. But we felt we could only go so far with a blunt-edge approach to CPD, mainly involving work with the whole staff together. While I don't like innovation for its own sake, when I became Headteacher, I decided that we would become a thinking school, and started a new journey that has been driven by one of the Deputy Headteachers.

(Headteacher)

We now have more personalised CPD rather than whole-school approaches. We have four consultants who are former senior leaders, who work with departments to connect departmental development with their own development. Research is the key to making staff reflect and improve their practice. Corina Seal has the brief for this. We have the MA programme, and over 40% of staff have done TLA. The piece of work they do at the end of the TLA stage is not necessarily the key thing but rather the process.

(Headteacher)

The School Development Plan sets priorities, and then a decision is taken whether or not to set up a Research and Development Group to work on each priority. These meet every two weeks. One has been meeting now for over a year, but they used to be of shorter duration. An example would be the group that worked on a whole-school approach to assessing students' progress. The consultants were involved in this; they asked students questions about target-setting, so the students were brought into the research process. Another example is the Virtual Learning Environment (VLE). This is being driven through a Research and Development Group linked to the TLA structure. The students are involved, and staff are trying things out: they go out and look at other schools. We want a balance between the abstract and practical aspects of research. Some staff do not value theory.

(Deputy Headteacher)

In my work with another school I wanted to look at high ability at KS4, and came up with a module of work which is now being taught. I observe classes working on the module and evaluate the outcomes every Friday. I shall write it up before the summer holiday.

(Head of Maths)

The comments above illustrate the central importance given to continuing professional development as the strategic driver of school improvement. Senior leadership resources have been deployed to that end, and significant internal and external support has been provided through the consultants, Master's programmes and the TLA. There is a strong planning framework in place, which uses the mechanism of 'research and development groups' to take forward key issues in the school development plan. In addition to these strong internal arrangements, the school also has an outward-looking orientation, illustrated by references to observing and supporting other schools.

5. How and to what extent does the leadership team ensure that practitioner research undertaken by staff is relevant to the interests and needs of other staff?

I do a lot of qualitative data collection, especially through interviews with teachers and students. The departments self-evaluate, then I gather data from teachers and students to support that. There is a shared framework for this.

(Consultant)

In addition to the representative comment above, it is clear that the selection of topics for research is undertaken collaboratively and that a range of mechanisms ensure its relevance to departmental and whole-school objectives.

6. How and to what extent does the leadership team encourage staff to work collaboratively?

There is an expectation of collaboration. This culture is an expectation school-wide.

(Head of Maths)

Collaboration is reinforced by linking research engagement to the departmental structure and to performance management, and by specific collaborative structures, such as the research and development groups.

C. Enabling

7. How and to what extent does the leadership team provide intellectual stimulation by drawing upon professional reading and published research findings?

This is illustrated by the following comments and by the earlier section on professional reading:

> *The Master's programme has been a good way to apply theory to practice. We talk with newly qualified teachers about the application of theory. People undertaking TLA get time with consultants and are encouraged to read. People watch Teachers' TV for example to plan initial teacher training sessions. We have a whole staff residential annually. Everyone comes on Friday, then the overnight stay and Saturday are optional. We get external input on the Friday, and then discuss and apply this on the Saturday.*
>
> (Advanced Skills Teacher)

> *I have had brilliant support: a mentor, my HOD and Heather with the TLA, so three people to turn to offering good support and guidance. I can go to any teacher for advice; it is a fantastic place to be for learning. The culture is led by the senior management, who are always looking for new ideas on teaching and learning, and these filter down. If teachers have ideas, they can bring them forward. The research and development meetings and workshops have different topics – people bring ideas – that has been led more by the head of department. The Headteacher keeps the staff very happy.*
>
> (NQT – Geography)

8. How and to what extent does the leadership team ensure that staff are given time to engage in practitioner research?

> *Continuing professional development has always been at the heart of our school improvement process. Ten years ago we wanted consistency, so there were a lot of whole-school CPD sessions, mainly delivered by the leadership team. Then, a more personalised learning approach became our priority and we thought how to do this for teachers. We needed to differentiate and to work in new ways, so we gave more time for departmental heads to do things.*
>
> (Deputy Headteacher)

Little direct reference was made to time being allocated specifically to support research engagement. This may in itself be a comment on how far the practice of research engagement has been institutionalised as a normal part of working practice.

9. How and to what extent does the leadership team ensure that staff are given time and opportunity to disseminate their practitioner research?

The work people do for TLA and the Master's modules has to be shared, for example in departmental meetings, and has to influence practice, for example by providing food for thought for teachers to consider their own practice.

(Consultant)

I went to courses, which the school supports, on outstanding lessons, using Kolb's theory of active learning. I applied it in lessons, and maths teaching is changing. I did that for a year and wrote it up as a TLA report. It was disseminated to the department and to the whole school in an after-school session, and at the residential as a Saturday morning workshop.

(Head of Maths)

So, we do our own learning. We share ideas in the departmental office, and we develop shared practice.

(Head of Maths)

10. How and to what extent does the leadership team enable staff engaged in practitioner research to develop their skills in sharing their results with colleagues?

This was not addressed directly, but it is clear that staff have opportunities to share their results in settings including departmental meetings. It is a reasonable assumption that having the opportunity to practise sharing results in supportive contexts, and hearing colleagues doing the same, would have the effect of developing both skills and confidence.

11. How and to what extent does the leadership team procure external support, e.g. from a university, for staff engaged in practitioner research?

TLA helped us a lot with research. It generated high energy, teachers wanted to try things, and TLA gave a structure for their learning. The leadership team decided that for themselves, participation in TLA would be compulsory and that for everyone else it would be optional. The staff drive it. It started small and snowballed.

(Deputy Headteacher)

Although the TLA tended to be foregrounded in these interviews, it was clear from other comments and information that the school has also been engaged significantly with Master's programmes which provide external university support for school-based enquiry.

Applying some definitions

Chapter 1 explored the question 'What is a research-engaged school?', by presenting and critiquing the pioneering definition of Handscomb and MacBeath (2003) and a later form offered by Sharp *et al.* (2006a), and by proposing the definition on which this book is based. Handscomb and MacBeath's first criterion (of four) is that 'significant decisions are informed by research, by this being built into organisational systems'. The fourth criterion (of five) defined by Sharp *et al.* is that the school 'uses evidence for decision-making'.

The following comments illustrate different ways in which research and decision-making are connected at Sweyne Park.

The comment below is an example of research being used to help to discern how to move forward in relation to a policy development:

> *When Every Child Matters came in, I led an audit. I think it is important to get people to come and tell you what they do and help them to reflect on it. I spent a lot of time with the head of the hearing impaired unit in this way.*
>
> (Consultant)

The following comment is an example of an enquiry-based approach being applied directly to management decision-making:

> *I did TLA looking at leadership roles and skills within the department and how tasks are assigned to different people. There are 13 staff in the department: a lot are young and need to develop, so I divided tasks and allocated them so as to develop their skills. So now members of the department have their areas of leadership, such as Key Stage 3, or Assessing Pupils' Progress (APP). I have learnt that in my role as a HOD I don't have to be the one doing everything: it is possible to share tasks with guidance. People want to take on extra tasks; for example one of the teachers wanted to take on the organisation of the curriculum days.*
>
> (Head of Science)

The comment below embraces three different examples: 'trying different approaches and evaluating findings' describes an action-research approach in which decision-making is integrated with cycles of experimentation and review; this is followed by an example of informed collaborative decision-making; and finally an example of research leading to a tangible new initiative:

> We have research and development meetings; we try different approaches and evaluate findings. We work collaboratively on how to enhance students' learning. We are all collaborative rather than managerial. I want everyone to be involved in the decision about a new syllabus for GCSE: all the information has been shared and we will reach a joint decision. I did the same when we took on a new Key Stage 3 syllabus. This way there is no resentment. A lot of research goes on, for example on girls in physics, which has involved girls going to the junior school to teach physics to the junior pupils.
>
> (Head of Science)

The first criterion suggested by Sharp *et al.* was that a research-engaged school 'investigates key issues in teaching and learning' (Sharp *et al.*, 2006a). Plenty of the comments recorded illustrated this criterion in operation at Sweyne Park, of which the following are representative examples:

> We always try to focus on the students' learning: we don't get distracted by issues of lower importance. Because the school grew out of two closing schools, we had to be a school where we focus on teaching and learning.
>
> (Consultant)

> The emphasis will be on progress: what my classes need from me as the head of department. I will feed back the research to the department. Lessons are changing so that the students are more independent; they include activities to remember skills rather than relying on repetition.
>
> (Head of Maths)

> Research has been a huge contributory factor to the excellent Ofsted judgement.
>
> (Consultant)

> The benefit to practice is evident in the examination results, lesson observations, activities involving students in their learning, and in assessment for learning, although there is more to do in that. What is done in lessons is deeper and riskier, and what the people observing lessons are commenting on has changed over the last three years: it is now much more perceptive. There are a lot of other examples of effects in departments.
>
> (Headteacher)

Conclusion

The comments presented above provide snapshots of an institution where a momentum has been established for a particular style of working in which research engagement features strongly. A factor in this has been the stability of staffing, which in turn has been assisted by the school's involvement in initial teacher education.

The very strong emphasis given to the engagement of students was discussed in Chapter 8, where the suggestion was made that there is a resonance between research engagement, the educative empowerment of the students, and the creation of a school which can truly be described as learning-centred.

Some readers may want to ask how much of these laudable activities can truly be described as 'research', as distinct, for example, from 'evidence-informed reflective practice'. The school's oral and written comments tend to bracket together 'research and development' or 'research and CPD' in ways that invite that question. When it was posed, the answer was: 'What we do isn't the same as academic research and we don't pretend that it is'. Graham Handscomb has commented that:

> Most teachers would not readily engage with the notion of being a 'teacher researcher'. A more helpful term...is teacher as enquirer. This alludes to teachers who are keen to reflect upon and critique their practices. They make good use of research and evidence to stimulate thinking...and then to evaluate the impact.
>
> (Handscomb, 2004: 95–6)

He commented on the range of views regarding the extent to which this activity 'counts' as research, including the view that there is a continuum on which 'evidence-informed practice' merges into 'research' (Handscomb, 2004). In Chapter 5 it was argued that 'research' has both a narrow technical meaning and a broader meaning in popular usage, so the same continuum could be seen as being between different but equally valid uses of the word 'research'. That continuum seemed to be present in microcosm at Sweyne Park, in that research projects assessed as part of Master's programmes certainly demonstrated academic rigour, while some of the other activity was of a broader 'enquiry' nature. Durrant and Holden (2006) turn the debate around: instead of asking how far teacher enquiry forms part of research, they offer a counter-perspective that research is only part of teacher enquiry – note the use of the word 'limits' in the following:

> We believe that school-based enquiry can be much more powerful if we can think beyond the limits of teacher research, focusing instead

on teachers' leadership of learning and the building of individual and collective capacity for school improvement.

(Durrant and Holden, 2006: 34)

As part of its own reflections, Sweyne Park School identified a series of four phases in its journey of research engagement, which are summarised in the box below. The phases that the school identified in its development are different from the developmental stages of researcher-leadership proposed in Chapter 6, although there are parallels between them, in that both describe increases in the spread of involvement across the school community, and increases in the significance of research engagement as a feature of the school's professional culture. Clearly, the leadership at Sweyne Park fulfils the characteristics of stage four ('Culture of practitioner research is fully institutionalised'), i.e. the most developed stage of school research engagement described in Chapter 6.

Phases of development at Sweyne Park School

Phase 1 (1997–2001): Establishing the culture

Several research strands were put in place from the outset, for example research and development groups and the use of student voice. The school was involved in large-scale academic research projects, including with Cambridge University, and staff in leadership and management positions were engaged in practitioner research, including through Best Practice Research Scholarships. Only staff in leadership and management positions were directly involved in research, but at this time a culture of sharing good practice was encouraged. The introduction of initial teacher education in 1999 reinforced the concept of every adult being a learner.

Phase 2 (2001–03): Expanding research activity within and beyond the school

The school increased its research activity through links, networks and international visits which were followed up in research and development groups. The school participated in the South Essex Networked Learning Community, and in the GTCE-funded Early Career project. A group was involved in the NCSL Research Lesson Study. Research findings were shared more widely and the growth of initial teacher education strengthened links with higher education institutions.

Phase 3 (2003–06): Incorporating varied research and CPD strands into a coherent structure

Personalised CPD was introduced as a scheme, encouraging staff to choose from a menu that included research lesson study, peer observation, consultant support and coaching days, fully involving all staff. Newly qualified and trainee staff were involved in research projects linked to Teachers TV resources and other small-scale research was incorporated into their training programmes. The school was chosen by CUREE as a case study in coaching and mentoring.

Phase 4 (2006 to present): Linking research more directly to students' learning

The Teacher Learning Academy was introduced across the school to support the concept of the 'Thinking School'. Additionally, some staff have been taking research-based Master's programmes. The school successfully bid for PPD development funds. Student involvement in the research community has expanded and the school has been involved in several national research projects, including the Specialist Schools and Academies Trust's Research Engaged Schools Project and Durham University's Plausible Estimation Project. Staff trained as TLA coaches and verifiers.

(Sweyne Park School)

References

Adler, P. and Adler, P. (1998) 'Observational techniques'. In N. Denzin and Y. Lincoln (eds), *Collecting and Interpreting Qualitative Materials*. Thousand Oaks: Sage.

Altheide, D. and Johnson, J. (1998) 'Criteria for assessing interpretive validity in qualitative research'. In N. Denzin and Y. Lincoln (eds), *Collecting and Interpreting Qualitative Materials*. Thousand Oaks: Sage.

Ambrose, D. (1987) *Managing Complex Change*. Pittsburgh: The Enterprise Group Ltd.

Anderson, G. and Herr, K. (1999) 'The new paradigm wars: Is there room for rigorous practitioner knowledge in schools and universities?'. *Educational Researcher*, 28(5).

Aspinwall, K. (1998) *Leading the Learning School*. London: Lemos & Crane.

Aspinwall, K. and Pedler, M. (1997) 'Schools as learning organisations'. In B. Fidler, S. Russell and T. Simpkins (eds), *Choices for Self-managing Schools*. London: Paul Chapman.

Bailey, R., Pearce, G., Winstanley, C., Sutherland, M., Smith, C., Stack, N. and Dickenson, M. (2008) *A Systematic Review of Interventions Aimed at Improving the Educational Achievement of Pupils Identified as Gifted and Talented*. Report No. 1612. London: EPPI-Centre, Social Science Research Unit, Institute of Education, University of London.

Bauer, S. and Brazer, S. (2012) *Using Research to Lead School Improvement: Turning evidence into action*. Thousand Oaks: Sage.

Bell, M., Cordingley, P., Isham, C. and Davis, R. (2010) *Report of Professional Practitioner Use of Research Review: Practitioner engagement in and/or with research*. Coventry: CUREE, GTCE, LSIS and NTRP. Online. <http://www.curee-paccts.com/node/2303> (accessed 10 January 2011).

Black, P. and Wiliam, D. (1998) *Inside the Black Box: Raising standards through classroom assessment*. London: King's College London.

Black-Hawkins, K. (2008a) 'Networking schools'. In C. McLaughlin, K. Black-Hawkins, D. McIntyre and A. Townsend (eds), *Networking Practitioner Research*. Abingdon: Routledge.

–– (2008b) 'Blackburn with Darwen leading into Networked Learning Community'. In C. McLaughlin, K. Black-Hawkins, D. McIntyre and A. Townsend (eds), *Networking Practitioner Research*. Abingdon: Routledge.

–– (2008c) 'South West London Networked Learning Community'. In C. McLaughlin, K. Black-Hawkins, D. McIntyre and A. Townsend (eds), *Networking Practitioner Research*. Abingdon: Routledge.

Bridges, D. (1997) 'Philosophy and educational research: A reconsideration of epistemological boundaries'. *Cambridge Journal of Education*, 27(2).

–– (1998) 'On conceptual analysis and educational research: A response to John Wilson'. *Cambridge Journal of Education*, 28(2).

–– (2006) *Insider and Outsider Research*. Online. <http://www.bera.ac.uk/ ethics-and-educational-research-philosophical-perspectives/> (accessed 25 July 2010).

British Educational Research Association (BERA) (2004) *Revised Ethical Guidelines for Educational Research*. Online. <http://www.bera.ac.uk> (accessed 25 July 2010).

Brittingham, K. (1999) 'The characteristics of successful school, family and community partnerships'. Paper presented at the American Educational Research Association Conference, Montreal, 19–23 April.

Budge, D. (2010) *Case Study on the Impact of IOE Research: The deployment and impact of support staff (DISS) project*. London: Institute of Education, University of London.

Burbules, C. and Torres, C. (2000) *Globalisation and Education: Critical perspectives*. New York: Routledge.

Burton, D. and Hartlett, S. (2005) *Practitioner Research for Teachers*. London: Paul Chapman.

Campbell, A. and Groundwater-Smith, S. (eds) (2007) *An Ethical Approach to Practitioner Research*. Abingdon: Routledge.

Caplan, N., Morrison, A. and Stambauch, R. (1975) *The Uses of Social Science Knowledge in Policy Decisions at the National Level*. Ann Arbor: University of Michigan Press.

Carr, W. and Hartnett, A. (1996) *Education and the Struggle for Democracy*. Buckingham: Open University Press.

Chiswell, K. (1995) 'How is action research helping to develop my role as a communicator?'. *British Educational Research Journal*, 21(3).

Cochran-Smith, M. and Lytle, S. (1998) 'Teacher research: The question that persists'. *International Journal of Leadership in Education*, 1, 19–36.

−− (2007) 'Everything's ethics: Practitioner inquiry and university culture'. In A. Campbell and S. Groundwater-Smith (eds), *An Ethical Approach to Practitioner Research*. Abingdon: Routledge.

Collarbone, P. (1997) 'A journey of a thousand miles: The Haggerstone journey'. In B. Davies and J. West-Burnham (eds), *Re-engineering and Total Quality in Schools*. London: Pitman.

Cordingley, P. (2004) 'Teachers using evidence: Using what we know about teaching and learning to reconceptualise evidence-based practice'. In G. Thomas and R. Pring (eds), *Evidence-based Practice in Education*. Maidenhead: Open University Press.

Crow, G. (2005) 'Developing leaders for schools facing challenging circumstances'. In M. Coles and G. Southworth (eds), *Developing Leadership*. Maidenhead: Open University Press.

CUREE (2010) *Route Map*. Centre for the Use of Research and Evidence in Education. Online. <http://www.curee-paccts.com> (accessed 21 December 2010).

Department for Children, Schools and Families (2008) *The Assessment for Learning Strategy*. Nottingham: DCSF Publications.

−− (2009) *The Lamb Inquiry – Special Educational Needs and parental confidence*. Nottingham: DCSF Publications.

Durrant, J. and Holden, G. (2006) *Teachers Leading Change: Doing research for school improvement*. London: Paul Chapman.

Edge, K., Frayman, K. and Lawrie, J. (2009) *The Influence of North-South School Partnerships: Final report executive summary*. London: Institute of Education, University of London.

Elliott, J. (1985) 'Educational action research'. In J. Nisbet, J. Megarry and S. Nisbet (eds), *World Yearbook of Education 1985: Research, policy and practice*. London: Kogan Page.

−− (1991) *Action Research for Educational Change*. Milton Keynes: Open University Press.

Elliott, J. and Doherty, P. (2001) 'Restructuring educational research for the Third Way?'. In M. Fielding (ed.), *Taking Education Really Seriously: Four years' hard Labour*. London: RoutledgeFalmer.

Epstein, J., Clark, L. and Van Voorhis, F. (1999) 'Two-year patterns of state and district leadership in developing programmes of school, family and community partnerships'. Paper presented at the American Educational Research Association Conference, Montreal, 19–23 April.

Epstein, J., Coates, L., Salinas, K., Sanders, M. and Simon, B. (1997) *School, Family and Community Partnerships: Your handbook for action*. Thousand Oaks: Sage.

Essex County Council (2009) *Active Enquiring Minds: Supporting young researchers*. Chelmsford: Forum for Learning and Research Enquiry (FLARE).

Finch, J. (1986) *Research and Policy: The uses of qualitative methods in social and educational research*. London: Falmer.

Fine, M. (1994) 'Dis-stance and other stances: Negotiations of power inside feminist research'. In A. Gitlin (ed.), *Power and Method: Political activism and educational research*. London: Routledge.

Frost, D. (1996) *Reflective Action Planning: A guide*. Canterbury: Canterbury Christ Church University College.

–– (2007) 'Practitioner research and leadership: The key to school improvement'. In A. Briggs and M. Coleman (eds), *Research Methods in Educational Leadership and Management*. London: Sage.

Frost, D. and Durrant, J. (2003) *Teacher-Led Development Work*. London: David Fulton.

Frost, D., Durrant, J., Head, M. and Holden, G. (2000) *Teacher-Led School Improvement*. London: RoutledgeFalmer.

Fullan, M. (1993) *Change Forces*. London: Falmer.

General Teaching Council for England (GTCE) (2006) *Using Research in Your School and Your Teaching*. Publication TPLF06. Birmingham: GTCE.

Goleman, D. (2000) 'Leadership that gets results'. *Harvard Business Review*, March–April.

Gouldner, A. (1965) 'Exploration in applied social science'. In A. Gouldner and S. Miller (eds), *Applied Sociology*. New York: Free Press.

Griffiths, M. (1998) *Educational Research for Social Justice: Getting off the fence*. Buckingham: Open University Press.

Guba, E. and Lincoln, Y. (1989) *Fourth Generation Evaluation*. Sage: London.

Halsall, R. (ed.) (1998) *Teacher research and school improvement*. Buckingham: Open University Press.

Hammersley, M. (1992) *What's Wrong with Ethnography? Methodological explorations*. London: Routledge.

–– (2002) *Educational Research, Policymaking and Practice*. London: Paul Chapman.

Handscomb, G. (2004) 'Collaboration and enquiry: Sharing practice'. In P. Earley and S. Bubb (eds), *Leading and Managing Continuing Professional Development*. London: Paul Chapman.

–– (2008) *Meaningful Self-evaluation: Using reflection for self-evaluation and the SEF*. Chelmsford: Essex County Council Forum for Learning and Research Enquiry (FLARE).

Handscomb, G. and MacBeath, J. (2003) *The Research Engaged School*. Chelmsford: Essex County Council Forum for Learning and Research Enquiry (FLARE).

Handscomb, G. and Smith, J. (2006) *Making Every Child Matter: The Essex LEArning Project*. Chelmsford: Essex County Council.

Hargreaves, D. (1996) *Teaching as a Research-Based Profession: Possibilities and prospects*. Teacher Training Agency Annual Lecture. London: Teacher Training Agency.

–– (1997) 'Respondent's comments'. In S. Hegarty (ed.), *The Role of Research in Mature Education Systems*. Slough: National Foundation for Educational Research.

–– (2001) 'Revitalising educational research: Past lessons and future prospects'. In M. Fielding (ed.), *Taking Education Really Seriously: Four years' hard Labour*. London: RoutledgeFalmer.

–– (2003) *Education Epidemic: Transforming secondary schools through innovation networks*. London: Demos.

Hellawell, D. (2000) 'Changes and challenges: An interview with Heather du Quesnay'. *Professional Development Today*, 4(1).

Hextall, I. and Mahoney, P. (1998) 'Effective teachers for effective schools'. In R. Slee and G. Weiner with S. Tomlinson (eds), *School Effectiveness for Whom?* London: Falmer.

Hillage, J., Pearson, R., Anderson, A. and Tamkin, P. (1998) *Excellence in Research on Schools*. London: Department for Education and Employment.

Holloway, I. (1997) *Basic Concepts for Qualitative Research*. Oxford: Blackwell Science.

Hopkins, D., Reynolds D. and Gray, J. (2005) *School Improvement: Lessons from research*. Nottingham: DfES Publications.

Hoyle, E. (1985) 'Educational Research: Dissemination, participation, negotiation'. In J. Nisbet, J. Megarry and S. Nisbet (eds), *World Yearbook of Education 1985: Research, policy and practice*. London: Kogan Page.

Husbands, C. (2011) 'Research and policy'. *Education Journal*, 127, 32.

Jackson, D. (2000) 'The school improvement journey: Perspectives on leadership'. *School Leadership and Management*, 20(1).

Johnson, S. (1996) *Leading to Change*. San Francisco: Jossey-Bass.

Johnston, C. and Caldwell, B. (2001) 'Leadership and organisational learning in the quest for world class schools'. *The International Journal of Educational Management*, 15(2).

Joyce, B., Calhoun, E. and Hopkins, D. (1999) *The New Structure of School Improvement*. Buckingham: Open University Press.

Keeble, H. and Kirk, R. (2007) 'Exploring the existing body of research'. In A. Briggs and M. Coleman (eds), *Research Methods in Educational Leadership and Management*. London: Sage.

Knoster, T., Villa, R. and Thousand, J. (eds) (2000) *Restructuring for Caring and Effective Education: Piecing the puzzle together*. Baltimore: Brookes.

Leahy, S. and Wiliam, D. (2009) 'From teachers to schools: Scaling up professional development for formative assessment'. Paper presented at the American Educational Research Association Conference, San Diego, April.

Leithwood, K., Janzi, D. and Steinbach, R. (1999) *Changing Leadership for Changing Times*. Buckingham: Open University Press.

Levin, B. (2001) *Reforming Education: From origins to outcomes*. London: RoutledgeFalmer.

Lynd, R. (1939) *Knowledge for What?* Princeton, NJ: Princeton University Press.

Mayer, S. (2009) 'Engagement in school-based collaborative enquiry'. *Professional Development Today*, 12(3).

–– (2010) 'Designing, building and engaging inquiry-based professional learning communities in schools: A case study of two pilot schools'. Conference paper presented at the International Congress for School Effectiveness and Improvement, Kuala Lumpur, 5–8 January.

McIntyre, D. (2008) 'Researching schools'. In C. McLaughlin, K. Black-Hawkins and D. McIntyre with A. Townsend (eds), *Networking Practitioner Research*. Abingdon: Routledge.

McLaughlin, C., Black-Hawkins, K., Brindley, S., McIntyre, D. and Taber, K. (2006) *Researching Schools: Stories from a schools-university partnership for educational research*. Abingdon: Routledge.

McLaughlin, C., Black-Hawkins, K., McIntyre, D. and Townsend, A. (2008) *Networking Practitioner Research*. Abingdon: Routledge.

McLean, A. (2003) *The Motivated School*. London: Paul Chapman.

McNiff, J. (1988) *Action Research: Principles and practice*. London: Routledge.

Middlewood, D. (1999) Chapters 6, 7 and 8 in D. Middlewood, M. Coleman and J. Lumby, *Practitioner Research in Education: Making a difference*. London: Paul Chapman.

Middlewood, D., Coleman, M. and Lumby, J. (1999) *Practitioner Research in Education: Making a difference*. London: Paul Chapman.

Mitchell, D. (1985) 'Research impact on educational policy and practice in the USA'. In J. Nisbet, J. Megarry and S. Nisbet (eds), *World Yearbook of Education 1985: Research, policy and practice*. London: Kogan Page.

Mockler, N. (2007) 'Ethics in practitioner research: Dilemmas from the field'. In A. Campbell and S. Groundwater-Smith (eds), *An Ethical Approach to Practitioner Research*. Abingdon: Routledge.

Morris, A. (2009) *Evidence Matters: Towards informed professionalism in education*. Reading: CfBT Education Trust.

Morris, A. and Peckham, M. (2006) *Final Report of the National Educational Research Forum*. NERF Working Paper 9.2. Online. <http://www.nerf-uk.org> (accessed 1 September 2009).

Moss, G. and Huxford, L. (2007) 'Exploring literacy policy-making from the inside out'. In L. Saunders (ed.), *Educational Research and Policy-Making*. Oxford: Routledge.

National College for School Leadership (NCSL) (2001) *Leading and Learning*. Nottingham: NCSL.

National Teacher Research Panel (NTRP) (2011) *Practitioner Summaries*. Online. <http://www.ntrp.org.uk/?q=node/4> (accessed 6 July 2011).

Newby, M. (1997) 'Educational action research: The death of meaning? Or the practitioner's response to utopian discourse'. *Educational Researcher*, 40(2).

Nolan, A. and Putten, J. (2007) 'Action research in education: Addressing gaps in ethical principles and practices'. *Educational Researcher*, 36(7), 401–7.

Pedler, M. and Aspinwall, K. (1996) *The Purpose and Practice of Organisational Learning*. Maidenhead: McGraw-Hill.

Popper, K. (1966) *The Open Society and its Enemies*. 5th edn. London: Routledge and Kegan Paul.

–– (1999) *All Life is Problem Solving*. London: Routledge.

Ranson, S. (1994) *Towards the Learning Society*. London: Cassell.

–– (ed.) (1998) *Inside the Learning Society*. London: Cassell.

Rea, J. and Weiner, G. (1998) 'Cultures of blame and redemption – When empowerment becomes control: Practitioners' views of the effective schools movement'. In R. Slee and G. Weiner with S. Tomlinson (eds), *School Effectiveness for Whom? Challenges to the school effectiveness and school improvement movements*. London: Falmer.

Sachs, J. (2007) 'Foreword'. In A. Campbell and S. Groundwater-Smith (eds), *An Ethical Approach to Practitioner Research*. Abingdon: Routledge.

Sanders and Simon (1999) 'Progress and challenges: Comparing elementary, middle and high schools in the National Network of Partnership Schools'. Paper presented at the American Educational Research Association Conference in Montreal, 19–23 April.

Saunders, L. (ed.) (2007) *Educational Research and Policy-Making*. Oxford: Routledge.

Selden, R. (1997) 'The impact of educational research'. In S. Hegarty (ed.), *The Role of Research in Mature Education Systems*. Slough: National Foundation for Educational Research.

Sharp, C., Eames, A., Sanders, D. and Tomlinson, K. (2005) *Postcards from Research-Engaged Schools*. Slough: National Foundation for Educational Research.

Sharp, C., Eames, A., Sanders, D. and Tomlinson, K. (2006a) *Leading a Research-Engaged School*. Nottingham: National College for School Leadership.

Sharp, C., Handscomb, G., Eames, A., Sanders, D. and Tomlinson, K. (2006b) *Advising Research-Engaged Schools: A role for local authorities*. Slough: National Foundation for Educational Research.

Shortland-Jones, B., Alderson, A. and Baker, R. (2001) 'Leadership for cultural change: Developing a community of learners in teacher education'. *International Electronic Journal for Leadership in Learning*, 5(10). Online. <http://www.ucalgary.ca/iejll/shortland-jones_alderson_baker> (accessed 31 March 2011).

Slavin, R. (2008) 'Education reform requires teachers to apply research-proven methods'. *Education Journal*, 110.

Somekh, B. (2010) 'The Collaborative Action Research Network: 30 years of agency in developing education action research'. *Educational Action Research*, 18(1).

Stenhouse, L. (1983) *Authority, Education and Emancipation*. London: Heinemann.

Stoll, L., MacBeath, J., Smith, I. and Robertson, P. (2001) 'The change equation: Capacity for improvement'. In J. MacBeath and P. Mortimore (eds), *Improving School Effectiveness*. Buckingham: Open University Press.

Stoll, L. and Seashore Louis, K. (eds) (2007) *Professional Learning Communities: Divergence, depth and dilemmas*. Maidenhead: Open University Press/McGraw-Hill.

Street, H. (ed.) (2005) *Secondary Leadership Paper Number 21: Teaching as a research informed profession*. Haywards Heath: National Association of Head Teachers.

Suissa, J. (2006) *Professional Ethics and Applied Ethics*. Online. <http://www.bera.ac.uk/ethics-and-educational-research-philosophical-perspectives/> (accessed 25 July 2010).

Suri, H. (2008) 'Ethical considerations in synthesising research: Whose representations?'. *Qualitative Research Journal*, 8(1), 62–73.

—— (2010) 'Methodologically Inclusive Research Synthesis (MIRS): A multi-paradigmatic framework'. Symposium paper presented at the annual meeting of the American Educational Research Association, Denver, 30 April–4 May.

Suri, H. and Clarke, D. (2009) 'Advancements in research synthesis methods: From a methodologically inclusive perspective'. *Review of Educational Research*, 79(1), 395–430.

Thomas, P. (1985) *The Aims and Outcomes of Social Policy Research*. London: Croom Helm.

Tooley, J. and Darby, D. (1998) *Educational Research: A critique*. London: Office for Standards in Education.

Turner, L. (1998) 'Turning around a struggling school: A case study'. In L. Stoll and K. Myers (eds), *No Quick Fixes: Perspectives on schools in difficulty*. London: Falmer.

UKIERI (2010) *Cluster School Partnerships*. Online. <http://www.ukieri.org/phaseonefocusarea_clusterschoolpartnerships.html> (accessed 5 July 2011).

Villa, R. and Thousand, J. (1995) *Quality Enhancement of Teaching and Learning: Making the LEAP*. Perth: Curtin University of Technology.

Weiss, C. (1986) 'The many meanings of research utilisation'. In M. Bulmer, K. Bunting, S. Blume, M. Carley and C. Weiss (eds) *Social Science and Social Policy*. London: Allen and Unwin.

White, J. and Barber, M. (eds) (1997) *Perspectives on School Effectiveness and School Improvement*. London: Institute of Education, University of London.

White, V. (2007) 'Schools research in the English Ministry of Education: An insider's view'. In L. Saunders (ed.), *Educational Research and Policy-Making*. Oxford: Routledge.

Whitty, G. (2007) 'Education(al) research and education policy-making: Is conflict inevitable?'. In L. Saunders (ed.), *Educational Research and Policy-Making*. Oxford: Routledge.

Wilkins, R. (1986a) 'Between politics and scholarship'. *Education*, 18 April, 365.

—— (1986b) 'Gaining insights from foreign studies: A catechism for review'. *Educational Management and Administration*, 14(1), 49–59.

—— (1987) 'London case studies revisited'. *Educational Management and Administration*, 15(3), 203–12.

—— (1988) 'Research and policy in teachers' organisations'. *Journal of Education Policy*, 3(2), 89–103.

—— (2000a) 'Practitioner research in LEA-directed INSET'. *Journal of In-Service Education*, 26(1), 99–113.

—— (2000b) 'School, family and community partnerships: Applying a US model to the UK'. *Education Through Partnership*, 4(2).

—— (2002) 'Practitioner research and perceptions of school leadership'. *Education Today*, 52(4), 29–36.

—— (2005) *Teaching Assistants and the School Workforce of Tomorrow: Developing school support staff through practice development groups*. London: The College of Teachers.

—— (2010) 'The global context of local school leadership'. In M. Coates (ed.), *Shaping a New Educational Landscape*. London: Continuum.

Wilkins, R. and Head, M. (2002) *How to Retain and Motivate Experienced Teachers*. Canterbury: Canterbury Christ Church University College.

Wilkins, R. and MacBeath, J. (2002) 'An introduction to the OECD PISA Report'. *Inform* (Leadership for Learning, University of Cambridge), 1.

Wilkins, R., Head, M., Taylor, M. and Keaveny, B. (2004) *Supporting and Utilising the Experience of Older Teachers*. London: General Teaching Council for England.

Wilson, J. (1998) 'Preconditions for educational research'. *Educational Research*, 40(2).

Wilson, J. and Wilson, N. (1998) 'The subject matter of educational research'. *British Educational Research Journal*, 24(3).

Wilson, R., Hemsley-Brown, J., Easton, C. and Sharp, C. (2003) *Using Research for School Improvement: The LEA's role.* Slough: National Foundation for Educational Research.

Winter, R. (1998) 'Finding a voice – thinking with others: A conceptualization of action research'. *Educational Action Research*, 6(1).

Yuen, P. and Cheng, Y. (2000) 'Leadership for teachers' action learning'. *The International Journal of Educational Management*, 14(5).